RUSSIA WITHOUT PUTIN

RUSSIA WITHOUT PUTIN

*Money, Power and the Myths
of the New Cold War*

Tony Wood

VERSO

First published by Verso 2018
© Tony Wood 2018

1 3 5 7 9 10 8 6 4 2

Verso
UK: 6 Meard Street, London W1F 0EG
US: 20 Jay Street, Suite 1010, Brooklyn, NY 11201

versobooks.com

Verso is the imprint of New Left Books

ISBN-13: 978-1-78873-124-9
ISBN-13: 978-1-78873-537-7 (EXPORT)
ISBN-13: 978-1-78873-126-3 (US EBK)
ISBN-13: 978-1-78873-127-0 (UK EBK)

British Library Cataloguing in Publication Data
A catalogue record for this book is available from the British Library

Library of Congress Cataloging-in-Publication Data
A catalog record for this book is available from the Library of Congress

Typeset in Garamond by Biblichor Ltd, Edinburgh
Printed in the USA by Maple Press, York, PA 17406

For my parents

Contents

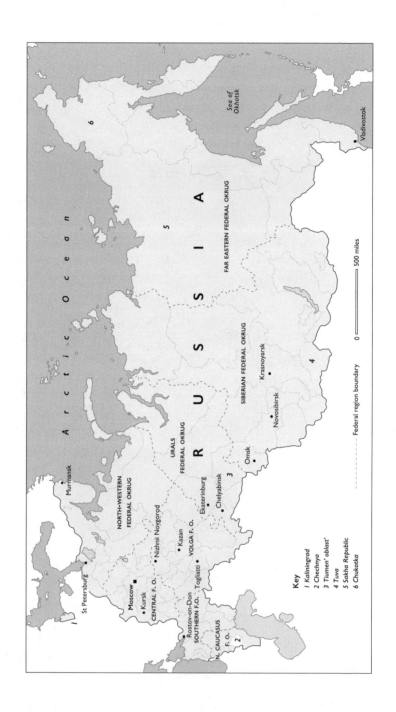

Introduction

I T IS HARD TO THINK of Russia today without thinking of Vladimir Putin. Perhaps more than any other major national leader, he personifies his country in the eyes of the outside world. In Russia itself, he has dominated the political scene for almost two decades with his trademark combination of cool calculation and prickly machismo, his every word beamed daily into homes across the country. And he has proved lastingly popular, sometimes attracting the kind of gushing admiration previously lavished on Communist leaders – a latter-day cult of personality expressed in fawning media coverage, kitschy memorabilia, even a brand of vodka. Through three presidential terms and two stints as prime minister, he has enjoyed approval ratings that would be the envy of any world leader. Since he first took office as Yeltsin's premier in August 1999, even surveys made by independent pollsters have rarely put him below 70 per cent, and he has largely remained above 80 since the spring of 2014, as tensions with the West have steadily mounted.

In the West, by contrast, perceptions of Putin have become increasingly negative. A drip feed of critical commentary from the mid-2000s onward gathered strength after the Russo-Georgian

War of 2008, and turned into a flood with the Ukraine crisis of 2013–14 and the start of Russia's intervention in Syria in 2015. Magazine covers and newspaper headlines, books and TV broadcasts more and more often depicted him as a twenty-first-century tsar, wielding absolute authority over his people. Meanwhile governments and NGOs alike pointed to one damning report after another on the human rights situation or the curtailment of journalistic freedoms in Russia. But this was nothing compared to the storm of vilification that has arisen since the 2016 US presidential elections, as allegations of Russian interference, influence-buying and collusion have dogged the Trump administration through its first year and beyond. Not since the days of Reagan has Russia seemed so central to US political life – and not since the depths of the Cold War has it been so unambiguously assumed across most of the political spectrum that Russia is the United States' principal enemy.

Yet despite the glaring mismatch between Western condemnation and domestic support, there has been general agreement on at least one thing: the absolute centrality of Vladimir Putin. In the West, Russia's president is portrayed as the most implacable foe of the US and its allies, a malevolent puppet master pulling the strings in a succession of crises across the world. In Russia, his supporters see him as inseparable from the fate of the country itself. In October 2014, his deputy chief of staff asserted sycophantically that 'there is no Russia today if there is no Putin'.[1] For his domestic detractors, too, he remains a focal point, though one of anger and frustration. In 2011–12, protesters dismayed at his impending return to the presidency adopted a slogan that in some ways simply turned the official Kremlin line inside out: '*Rossiia bez Putina*' – 'Russia without Putin'.

By themselves, these three words might be read as a straightforward call for regime change. That is not at all the intention of this book. My argument, rather, is that Western media coverage and analysis of Russia are overly fixated on Putin's personality.

Time and again, the characteristics of the man are used to explain the behaviour or interests of the state. The conflation is to some extent understandable: Russia is a country in which political power is not only highly concentrated but deeply personalized, so the preferences and whims of the figure at the very heart of the system take on an outsized importance. But even in an age when it has become common to analyse complex events through the prism of singular personalities, the recurrent focus on Putin has become particularly extreme. And it is unhelpfully self-confirming: the more media coverage and analysis uses him to explain Russia, the more Putin comes to dominate, constantly narrowing our frame of reference.

Too much attention has been paid to the man, and not enough to the system over which he presides. The obsession with Putin's persona effectively reduces a whole range of political, economic and social questions to the swings of one individual's mood or morality. At best, this is highly misleading, distracting us from the broader structural forces that have done so much to shape Russia's fortunes in the last few decades. At worst, the focus on Putin is dangerously counter-productive, leading to profoundly mistaken ideas about the source of Russia's ills. The notion that a single person is responsible for everything that happens in Russia shades all too readily into the belief that changing the figure at the top will rectify the problem. Putin did not create the system, nor will his removal from the scene alter its fundamental character. In order to understand Russia today, the West needs to shake off its obsession with Putin and look at what lies beyond the Kremlin walls. It needs, in other words, to learn to see Russia without Putin.

At a time when Russia has moved to the centre of public debate in much of the West, it is especially important to have a more informed idea of what the country is actually like. At the height of the Cold War, Western views of the USSR often came packaged in pat formulas about tyranny and freedom, totalitarianism versus democracy. But at least there was a sizeable body of writers, scholars, activists and thinkers who could supply a more nuanced perspective, based on first-hand experience. The West's levels of expertise and awareness about Russia have, sadly, declined steeply since then, opening the way for all kinds of ill-informed speculation – often churned out by individuals with no knowledge of the place, let alone of the people or the language – to circulate unchallenged. As a result, public opinion and policy decisions are based on a very shallow understanding of the country.

The purpose of this book is to provide a portrait of contemporary Russia that goes beyond the blaring headlines about its president. How is Russia ruled, and for whose benefit? What are the consequences for Russian society? How can we best explain Russia's mounting clashes with the West? Where is the country headed? To answer these questions, we need to discard several of the core assumptions behind most discussions of Putin's Russia.

First, there is the widespread notion that Putin has overseen a nostalgic return to Soviet times, reversing the market reforms and democratization carried out by Yeltsin in the 1990s. Second, the idea that Putin and a small clique around him control and decide everything in Russia, constituting a 'kleptocracy' or 'mafia state'. Third, the belief – shared by many Russians, too – that the country's problems can in large part be put down to the lingering legacies of the Soviet past; with the logical follow-on that as and when these legacies are shed, Russia will be able to join the ranks of 'normal' capitalist countries. A fourth key trope of Western analysis is to blame the relative weakness of the opposition on a combination of Soviet holdovers and Putin's authoritarianism – in other words, on apathy from below and repression from above. Finally, in the realm of foreign policy, there is the conviction that Russia under Putin has become an aggressor state, bent on a return to Cold War–style confrontation with the West, or even on the destruction of Western democracy itself.

The chapters that follow overturn each of these assumptions. Far from destroying the legacies of Yeltsin's neoliberal restructuring,

Putin in many crucial ways preserved and extended them. There are, to be sure, differences between the style and temperament of the two leaders, but there has been no fundamental change in the character of the system itself. Indeed, the 1990s and 2000s should be seen as two phases in the evolution of the same system: first, a turbulent period in which the Soviet order was destroyed and a new capitalist model installed – with enthusiastic backing from the West – followed by a period of stabilization and consolidation, as the new model sank its roots deep into the country's socio-economic soil. Throughout, the system's main priority has been to defend capitalism in Russia – if necessary at the expense of democracy, as the consistent resort to electoral rigging, from the 1990s to the present, demonstrates. The authoritarianism for which Putin is widely criticized is not the product of any sinister personal preference, but rather an integral feature of the system he inherited and has continued.

Much Western commentary since the mid-2000s has decried Russia's apparent turn away from the free-market reforms of the 1990s toward a statism that has in practice tended to favour a select group at the top. Since 2014, many of these individuals, increasingly identified as 'kleptocrats', have been targeted by Western sanctions. Yet the corruption and rapacity of Russia's current rulers is nothing new, nor is it confined to a small clique. Many of Putinism's worst features are rooted in the socio-economic order that has been in place since the fall of Communism – embedded in the very form capitalism has taken in post-Soviet Russia. A closer look at the emergence and evolution of the Russian elite shows that power and wealth have been consistently interwoven since the USSR's collapse. From the outset, the installation of capitalism in Russia was dependent on the deliberate political decisions of the state, which set about creating a class of wealth-owners by handing out pieces of the planned economy at absurdly low prices. After 2000, the terms of the relationship between the state and private wealth began to change, but the state's commitment to the principle of private gain – and to the tremendous inequalities it generated – did not.

The weight of the Soviet past has repeatedly been invoked to explain the problems Russia faces in the present – from the authoritarian mind-set of the Putin government to endless bureaucracy to crumbling infrastructure. Behind this cliché lies the assumption that Russia's transition to capitalism has been stalled or even reversed by the persistence of Communism's legacies. This idea needs to be turned on its head: in the social realm, far from being an obstacle or burden, the Soviet past was a boon for Russia's post-Soviet rulers. After the collapse of the USSR, Russian society underwent a wrenching transformation, as a new, market-driven system of class inequalities emerged from the ruins of Soviet-era hierarchies. These two structures, old and new, then existed in parallel. The persistence of Communist-era social infrastructure alongside the emergent capitalist system was in many cases what allowed ordinary Russians to survive the 'transition' of the 1990s – giving the market-based order critical breathing room and helping to muffle discontent. Yet this parallelism of old and new is by definition a temporary phenomenon, and the hidden subsidy provided to the present by the Soviet past will inevitably run out. When it does, Russia's rulers may find themselves facing more unrest than they expected.

The protests of 2011–12 were the most serious internal challenge the Kremlin has faced this century, and were greeted in the Western media at the time as the 'beginning of the end' for Putin. Why did that hasty verdict prove so unfounded, and how do we explain the overall weakness of opposition movements in Russia today? The sheer power of the Kremlin relative to its opponents is certainly a major part of the answer. But the character of the opposition itself – its internal divisions and weaknesses – also played a role. If we look beyond the demonstrations of 2011–12, to the constellation of smaller protests that preceded and followed them, we can see a persistent gap between those calling for political reforms to the existing system and the broader, ideologically more diverse movements seeking to address the social consequences of Putin's rule. Western coverage tends to focus on the problem of who might stand a chance of replacing Putin as president; in the past few years it has devoted a great deal of attention to anti-corruption campaigner Aleksei Navalnyi as a possible contender for the role. Yet any substantive change in the way Russia is ruled would involve much more than undoing Putin's personal power. It would mean bridging the gap between the opposition movement's political and social wings, in order to create a genuine alternative to the Putin system as a whole.

Heightened tensions within Russia have coincided with a dramatic worsening of relations with the West. This is often put down to an ingrained hostility to the West among Putin and the ruling elite, itself supposedly rooted in lingering Soviet-era prejudices. Yet a survey of Russia's foreign policy since the fall of Communism reveals a different picture. For much of the post-Soviet era, the Russian elite – Putin very much included – were committed to an ideal of alliance or even integration with the West. Over time, however, it became increasingly clear that this was a one-sided fantasy, and Russia's elite gradually abandoned it, swapping dreams of integration for a more strident defence of Russian interests.

This change in attitude did not take place because of any regression to Soviet thinking. It was driven, rather, by the underlying dynamic of relations between Russia and the West, which since the end of the Cold War have been characterized by a stark imbalance of power. Russia's weakness after 1991 freed the West – the US in particular – to pursue its own strategic designs, foremost among them the expansion of NATO. In the face of Western dominance, Russia was compelled to accept these moves as *faits accomplis*. This profound asymmetry was always likely to generate resentment and tension, and sure enough, conflicts developed between Russia and the West over Kosovo in 1999 and 2007–08 and over Georgia in 2008. But it was only with the Ukraine crisis and annexation of Crimea in 2013–14 that Russia finally dropped the idea of alliance with the West – a development that places us on the other side of a major geopolitical watershed.

This has raised with renewed urgency the question of Russia's place in the world. Now that the Russian fantasy of integration with the West has crumbled, the country once again finds itself confronting a series of large-scale dilemmas. Where is Russia going, and what role might it play in the twenty-first century? What are the internal dynamics and external forces that are likely to constrain its choices? Demographic trends – including substantial inward and outward migration as well as a simultaneous aging and dwindling of the population – and the economy's increasing tilt toward natural-resource exports will reshape Russian society in complex and unpredictable ways. At the same time, the country faces a contentious and competitive global environment, in which it will likely occupy a less prosperous and prominent position. Yet it will, for all that, remain a significant player, with considerable resources at its disposal. Much hinges, in the end, on how it chooses to use them, and for whose benefit.

The answers to these questions depend in turn on the fate of the political system currently in place. Putin's victory in the March 2018 presidential election was such a foregone conclusion that, long before the vote itself, many minds in Russia were already turning to 2024, when he will once again reach the constitutional limit of two consecutive terms. What, they wondered, will happen when he finally leaves office? Behind the question of Putin's personal fate lies the larger issue of how the system he presides over will fare. Are his whims and personality so closely bound up with it that his departure would be enough to bring it tumbling to the ground?

These kinds of speculation share with most Western discussions of contemporary Russia a tendency to credit Putin with an almost demiurgic power, as if he had constructed the system from scratch – fashioning it according to his desires the way a spider weaves its web. But the system is much less Putin's individual creation than the cumulative outcome of Russia's post-Communist transformations. And though he has undeniably had a strong influence on the way the system operates, some version of it is likely to far outlast Putin himself. What this means in turn is that we need to look beyond Putin to understand what that system is, how it really works, and what its consequences are for Russia and for the wider world.

CHAPTER 1

The Man and the System

W HO IS VLADIMIR PUTIN? And what can his personal background and experiences tell us about the country he has governed for close to two decades? There is a strange disproportion in the ever-expanding literature on the man: although a great deal has been published about him, we still know relatively little about his inner life, especially compared with other major global leaders.[1] He is both ubiquitous and elusive, a permanent public presence whose private world remains largely closed off. Still, there are a fair number of clues. The basic facts of his biography are well known, and were laid out in *First Person*, a book of autobiographical interviews published shortly after he became president in 2000. Surprisingly, almost two decades on, this carefully crafted document remains the principal source on his early life and career.[2]

Born in 1952 in what was then Leningrad, Putin grew up in a communal apartment with his working-class parents – his father was a wounded war veteran, his mother a factory worker. He himself recalls the tough milieu of the *dvor*, the courtyard between apartment blocks where childhood arguments were often decided by shoves or fistfights. Putin's readiness to see insults, a kind of constant, coiled defensiveness, has often been traced back to lessons learnt on Leningrad's streets. As a boy, he dreamed of becoming a spy. Cult Soviet TV programmes such as *Shchit i mech* (Shield and Sword) painted a romanticized picture of intelligence agents, and Putin claims he grew up wanting to imitate the exploits of the programme's undercover hero. After studying law at Leningrad State University from 1970–75, Putin joined the KGB and worked for the agency for several years in his native city, then spent a year at the Red Banner Institute, the KGB's intelligence academy in Moscow, from 1984–85.

In 1985, he was posted to Dresden, where by his account he carried out 'the usual intelligence activities: recruiting sources of information, obtaining information, analysing it, and sending it to Moscow.' The four and a half years he spent in the GDR were ones of dizzying change in the USSR, as Gorbachev's *perestroika* launched a far-reaching process of reform. In retrospect it seems significant that Putin missed this time of political and cultural ferment – the brief window when it still seemed possible that the old system could gradually be changed for the better. Eventually, though, the reforms – and in particular the economic situation – escaped the Communist Party's control, culminating in the disintegration of the Soviet Union at the end of 1991.

In the meantime, the USSR had withdrawn its support for the Communist regimes of the Eastern Bloc, which toppled one after another in the closing months of 1989. Putin, who shared a building in Dresden with members of the Stasi, saw these events unfold with alarm. He recounts burning papers 'night and day' and confronting a hostile crowd outside the door of his workplace. In the view of many experts, this experience led him to associate mass politics with the threat of disorder – a connection that might explain his apparent fear that Russia would be contaminated by the 'Colour Revolutions' that overthrew a string of post-Soviet regimes in the mid-2000s. (The same repulsion was evident in the Kremlin's virulent response to the Maidan protests in Ukraine in

2013–14.) There can be no doubt, in any event, that the fall of Communism was profoundly disorientating for Putin. Perhaps most bewildering of all was the lack of instructions or communications from Moscow. 'I got the feeling then', he later recalled, 'that the country no longer existed. That it had disappeared.'[3]

Putin has famously spoken of the fall of the USSR as a 'geopolitical catastrophe'. Along with many other Russians of his generation, he seems to have felt keenly the sense of national humiliation that the Soviet collapse brought; one of his former spin doctors has described Putin as part of 'a very extensive, but politically opaque, unrepresented, unseen layer of people who after the end of the 1980s were looking for *revanche*'.[4] The resentment only increased during the 1990s, when the former superpower found itself mired in endless economic crises and political turbulence, and the state apparatus turned into a chaotic jumble of factions. But this lingering bitterness was not the only thing that defined Putin's experience of the 1990s: the time he spent in the murky, overlapping realms of post-Soviet government and business also shaped his perceptions of how the new capitalist system really worked.

Putin returned to Leningrad in March 1990, and soon began working for his former law professor Anatoly Sobchak, first at the university and then in the city government. Sobchak was elected mayor in June 1991, at the same moment that the city switched its name back to St Petersburg. Putin was effectively Sobchak's deputy, and was placed in charge of the city's Committee for External Relations, making him the point of contact for all the foreign businesses rushing to make deals on one of capitalism's newest frontiers. The Soviet planned economy had been smashed, and almighty struggles – sometimes literal gunfights – were unfolding over the pieces. The state's grip on its economic infrastructure, its resources, even its borders had become shaky, and huge profits were being made from a whole range of illicit activities, from smuggling to extortion, from fraud to the seizure of state assets.

As one of the functionaries responsible for St Petersburg's economy, Putin issued licenses to thousands of new businesses, and saw for himself how the grey area of legality left behind by the state's collapse was creating fortunes for a sharp-elbowed few. He later described his role, euphemistically, as having to 'solve a fairly large number of problems and tasks of interest to various business structures'.[5] The city itself joined in the market free-for-all, forming dozens of joint-venture enterprises – one of which, overseen by Putin, involved a 51 per cent stake in all St Petersburg's casinos, and apparently resulted in millions of dollars in cash being funnelled into private pockets rather than the city's coffers.[6]

St Petersburg was desperately short of money at the time, but it did have plenty of raw materials – timber, oil, metals – so Putin devised a scheme to exchange these for much-needed food imports. But the food never arrived. This gave rise to a scandal that sheds light both on Putin's methods and on the priorities of the system in which he was operating.[7] According to a 1992 investigation led by Marina Salye, a member of the city council, there were serious irregularities in Putin's scheme, which involved $92 million worth of contracts. This included enormous commissions – kickbacks allegedly worth a total of $34 million. Salye's report was forwarded to the Russian Account Chamber, with the recommendation that Putin be dismissed, but no further action was taken. This was largely thanks to Sobchak, who apparently insisted the case be dropped. Putin himself later claimed he had been duped by the companies involved. But even on this generous reading, his oversight resulted in millions of dollars' worth of resources being drained from the city at a time when many of its inhabitants were virtually starving. At worst, he had potentially been involved in a far more deliberate and cynical plan for private enrichment at the public expense. Either way, Sobchak kept him in the job.

A further aspect of this episode is revealing in retrospect: several of the people in the St Petersburg city administration who rallied to Putin's defence in 1992 went on to play key roles in his regime after 2000. They included future president and prime minister Dmitri Medvedev; Pyotr Aven, who would become a prominent banker; the future justice and interior minister Sergei Stepashin; and the future head of the Russian Security Service (FSB) Nikolai Patrushev. Other figures with whom Putin forged important ties in the early 1990s include Igor Sechin, his aide in the city administration and later head of the state oil company, Rosneft; Matthias Warnig, a former Stasi officer who ran Dresdner Bank's new St Petersburg branch – the first foreign bank to operate in the city; and the businessmen Yuri Kovalchuk, Gennady Timchenko and Vladimir Yakunin, who all signed lucrative contracts with the city on Putin's watch.[8]

Personal connections like these are crucial to understanding how Russia works.[9] In the Soviet period, informal influence, or *blat* – translated as 'pull' – often dictated access to scarce goods, housing or coveted jobs. Its use was widespread because it was so essential to getting by. What was distinctive about the way *blat* came to function in the 1990s, however, was that personal connections were increasingly used as a means of making money. Previously a way for ordinary people to get around the inadequacies of the planned economy, they now served the powerful, blurring the lines between state office and private enrichment, and entangling the formal rules of government in a web of informal connections. In Russia, in any contest between legality and personal loyalties, the latter have generally won out. As we will see, Putin's entire career, from the 1992 food scandal to the present, is in some ways an illustration of this basic rule of post-Soviet politics.

In the summer of 1996, Putin briefly found himself at a loose end after Sobchak failed in his mayoral re-election bid. But Aleksei Kudrin, a former St Petersburg colleague working in Moscow – he would go on to be Putin's finance minister from 2000 to 2011 – soon recommended him for a post in Yeltsin's presidential administration, as deputy head of the Presidential Property Management Department. This was a highly sensitive role, placing him not only in charge of a sizeable portfolio of assets but also in the midst of a knot of crooked dealings. For example, one scandal over contracts with the Swiss construction firm Mabetex ultimately led to the arrest of his direct superior, Pavel Borodin, for money laundering in New York in 2001.

A virtual unknown in Moscow before his arrival, Putin proved adept at navigating the byzantine paths of Kremlin politics and, perhaps more important, showed a marked personal loyalty to his bosses and patrons. This quality no doubt smoothed his progress through the ranks of the Yeltsin administration, earning him promotion by March 1997 to head of the presidency's Main Control Directorate (GKU), which monitored the implementation of executive decisions. In May 1998, he was given another sensitive job in the presidential administration, in charge of the Kremlin's relations with Russia's regions. He had barely started when he was switched in July to a much more prominent role: director of the FSB, successor agency to the KGB.

What part had the KGB itself played in Putin's phenomenal ascent? Putin himself has said that, though he left the agency in 1990 when he returned to Leningrad, he remained in its 'active reserve' until August 1991, when a group of hardliners led by the KGB's chief made a coup attempt against Gorbachev. At this point, Putin claims, he formally resigned. This interval is, of course, when he began working for Sobchak. There is some debate about whether the job itself was arranged for him by the agency, as a kind of mission to supervise one of the country's rising politicians. Sobchak supposedly knew of Putin's KGB connections, but thought they might prove useful.

Does this mean that the agency's shadowy hand was also behind the rest of his career? Putin himself has done little to discourage the idea: in December 1999, not long after he became prime minister, he made a tongue-in-cheek announcement at a dinner commemorating the founding of the Soviet secret police: 'I would like to report that the group of FSB officers dispatched to work secretly in the federal government has been successful in the first set of assignments.' Six years later, in December 2005, he told another audience of FSB officers that 'there is no such thing as a former KGB man'.

Yet these statements are part of an image Putin has deliberately cultivated, and taking them at face value means buying into the mystique he was trying to create. He himself never went especially far within the KGB's ranks, and was never given the kind of sensitive, high-risk assignments that he had aspired to as a boy; he remained something of an outsider in the Soviet spy world. The main achievement of his time as head of the FSB was a drastic downsizing that cut staff at the organization's headquarters, the Lubyanka, by a third – scarcely the behaviour of a man bent on restoring the might of his alma mater.[10] Putin's KGB training and years of work within the institution would undoubtedly have given him certain skills and encouraged particular habits of mind. But perhaps equally important, in the context of his political career, are the similarities between secret-police methods and the routine practices of post-Soviet business: the use of blackmail and compromising information – *kompromat* – to apply pressure; manipulation of the legal system; consistent use of threatened or actual violence. In short, many of the features of Putin's Russia that have been traced to some shadowy KGB conspiracy were widespread under Yeltsin; indeed, they created the environment in which Putin came to power.

If Putin's ascent up to mid-1998 was remarkably rapid, the elevation that followed was almost shocking in its suddenness. In August 1999, a man of whom few Russians had even heard was appointed prime minister. At the time, the Yeltsin government was lurching from one crisis to the next, and Putin was its fifth premier in the space of a year. The fallout from the rouble collapse of 1998, when financial contagion from the Asian Crisis spread to Russia and eventually prompted a panicked currency devaluation, was one cause of the continued political instability. But just as important was Yeltsin's search for a reliable successor who would guarantee him immunity from prosecution after leaving office. It had become clear that Evgeny Primakov, who served as prime minister from September 1998 to May 1999, was not going to oblige. Worse still, Primakov showed signs of wanting to investigate irregularities in the privatization process Yeltsin had forced through a few years earlier. Primakov's successor, Sergei Stepashin – one of Putin's colleagues from St Petersburg – lasted barely three months before being discarded because he lacked the charisma to be a plausible presidential figure.

When Yeltsin designated the apparently quiet, colourless Putin, many Russians initially thought he, too, would be a mere place-holder. But behind closed Kremlin doors, the coterie around Yeltsin, known as The Family, had already decided Putin would play a much more significant role. Here Putin's loyalty to his patrons was decisive: he could be relied upon to shield Yeltsin and his clique from prosecution. Sure enough, one of the first measures he took as acting president, in the first hours of the year 2000 after Yeltsin unexpectedly stepped down, was to sign a decree guaranteeing the ex-president immunity. The founding act of Putin's presidency was an elite pact designed to shield his predecessor from prosecution.

But fidelity to Yeltsin did not in itself make his rise to supreme office inevitable. A broad public consensus behind Putin's candidacy still had to be forged. It was the Second Chechen War that, in a matter of weeks, transformed Putin from mere cypher to president-in-waiting. In late August 1999, an incursion into Dagestan by Chechen Islamist warlord Shamil Basaev and his troops, followed by a series of bombings of apartment buildings elsewhere in Russia, provided the pretext for Russia to launch another invasion of the separatist republic in the North Caucasus. The First Chechen War, unleashed by Yeltsin in December 1994, had ended in August 1996 in an ignominious stalemate, seen at the time as definitive proof of the decline of Russia's power. Its army had been fought to a standstill by bands of separatist fighters while images of senseless destruction streamed into living rooms across the country. Russian bombers had turned the Chechen capital, Grozny, into a sea of rubble and caused tens of thousands of civilian deaths.

Three years on, a key part of Putin's popular appeal was his commitment to reversing the humiliation inflicted in the North Caucasus – famously summed up in his vow to 'wipe out' Chechen separatists 'in the outhouse'. Warmly endorsed by the major Western powers, the assault on Chechnya – labelled an anti-terrorist operation – provided the springboard for Putin's rise to the Kremlin, sending his approval rating from a mere 31 per cent in August 1999 to 80 per cent three months later.

The Chechen campaign was the stage on which Putin tested and developed his presidential persona. This took time to emerge fully. It is striking now to watch footage of his first address to the nation as acting president, on New Year's Eve of 1999. Putin speaks haltingly, as if unprepared or lacking in conviction; but beneath the stilted delivery, there is a determination that would not have escaped viewers' attention. His sobriety, too, is in stark contrast to the rambling, drunken incoherence of Yeltsin's speech that same evening. Putin's low-key style was well received by much of the Russian public, who had grown tired of the high-sounding but empty rhetoric of the 1990s' politicians.

Putin also spoke clearly, and for the most part in the idiom of a well-educated person. In this he was unlike both Yeltsin and Gorbachev, who like many Communist-era Party bosses had accents that bespoke their proletarian or peasant origins. Putin's language was more that of a bureaucrat or manager, replete with technical-sounding euphemisms ('business structures') and references to 'solving problems'. His occasional swerves into street language – these became cruder and more frequent when he was under pressure – may have alarmed some in the liberal intelligent-sia. But they were often excused or even admired by others, seen as glints of steel amid the clouds of phrase-mongering offered by other politicians.

The story of Putin's ascent tells us a certain amount about the man who would come to dominate Russia after 2000. But for understanding how he would then rule, perhaps more important than his personal trajectory is the context in which his rise took place. The consensus that carried him to the presidency in March 2000 was to a large extent a negative one. Putin's initial success was founded less on a positive evaluation of what he was than on approval of what he was not: he emerged as an apparent alternative to Yeltsin and the other leading politicians of the 1990s. His candidacy required him to do very little. In fact, the less he committed himself to particular positions, the more the public could project onto him their own assumptions and desires. This is why Putin's rule, in its early stages, was marked by a kind of ideological weightlessness – and why, even as he took supreme office, Russians and foreigners alike still knew little about him. Putin was an empty centre around which all of Russia could be made to turn.

Both at the time and since, Putin has been widely perceived as marking a sharp break with what came before. Yet this overlooks the extent to which he represented a continuation of Yeltsin – a fact summed up symbolically in the guarantee of immunity he gave his predecessor on taking office, and in the quasi-monarchical succession through which he gained the presidency. Indeed, though a great deal changed in Russia after 2000, in crucial respects the political and economic arrangements that took shape during the 1990s were maintained and consolidated.

On the face of it, the Zero Years – as the 2000s are known in Russia – seemed markedly different from what had come before. Yeltsin's erratic improvisation gave way to the cold calculation personified in Putin. After a decade in which the state apparatus had been hollowed out, Putin now began to reassert its authority. The tone was set early on by his frequent mentions of the 'vertical of power'. The country's parliament came increasingly to be dominated by the pro-Putin United Russia party, founded in 2001. In stark contrast to the constitutional free-for-all of the 1990s, when many of Russia's territorial subunits laid claim to extensive powers, Putin established a clear chain of command, firmly subordinating Russia's regions to Moscow by appointing plenipotentiaries to head seven new federal superdistricts, the *okrugá*. In the media, the boisterous, incoherent pluralism of the Yeltsin years was replaced after 2000 by a solid, at times deadening consensus, as the Kremlin gained control over the main TV networks and brought the more critical media outlets to heel.

Economically, the prolonged post-Soviet collapse was followed by recovery after the 1998 rouble crash, and then by an oil-fuelled boom in the new century. After reaching a nadir of $9 per barrel in mid-1998, the price of Urals crude oil more than doubled by 2002, and then rose past $50 by 2005, before rocketing to $138 in mid-2008.[11] This underwrote a period of impressive growth in Russia, with GDP increasing by an annual average of close to 7 per cent in Putin's first presidential term, and almost 8 in his second. Taxes on hydrocarbon exports filled state coffers again, enabling the government to pay wage and pension arrears. Real incomes rose by an average of more than 10 per cent a year in the first half of the decade, poverty levels dropped from 30 per cent in 2000 to just under 18 per cent in 2004, and unemployment shrank from its 1998 peak of 13 per cent to 6 per cent by 2007.[12]

Yet despite these differences, there were deeper continuities between the Russia of Yeltsin and that of Putin. Politically, the system that prevailed in the 2000s was not a perversion of Yeltsinism but its maturation. Lauded in the West as the architect of democracy in Russia, Yeltsin showed little respect for its principles in practice. In October 1993, faced with a fractious legislature – the Congress of People's Deputies elected in 1990 – he sent tanks to shell it into submission, and then rewrote the constitution, increasing the president's powers exponentially; the changes were approved by a rigged referendum in December. Even before that, he had sidestepped democratic accountability by implementing much of the key legislation that shaped the post-Soviet economy through a series of decrees; some of them, notably on privatization, were drafted by Western advisers. In Chechnya, Yeltsin moved to crush local aspirations to sovereignty, unleashing total war against the civilian population in 1994.

On each of these fronts, Putin continued what Yeltsin had begun. Yeltsin had put the national legislature in its place in 1993, but in the wake of the 1998 rouble crisis the Duma had again showed signs of rebellion. Putin brought it firmly back under control, streamlining the party system so that by 2007 there were only three parties to manage besides the ruling United Russia. One of them, A Just Russia, was the Kremlin's own confection, set up in 2006 to siphon votes from the Communist Party (KPRF). There was hardly any need, though, since the KPRF and the nationalist LDPR (the wildly misnamed Liberal Democratic Party of Russia) didn't constitute much of an opposition: on most significant issues they rubber-stamped the government's legislation. In December 2003, Boris Gryzlov, the Duma chairman, summed up the legislature's negligible role by declaring, 'Parliament is not a platform for political battles.'[13] Having reined in regional elites by appointing plenipotentiaries over their heads, in 2004 Putin further restricted their autonomy by abolishing elections for governors and mayors (though these were partially reintroduced in 2012).

The waging of war in Chechnya was central to Putin's rise, not only boosting his image early on, but also creating a diffuse sense of threat that served to rally public opinion around the leader. But here again, Putin was following in Yeltsin's footsteps, having digested the lessons of the First Chechen War. Russia's second invasion was still more ruthless than the first, levelling what was left of Grozny. Putin had also noted the vital role played by the media in sustaining opposition to the first conflict. This time, journalists trying to report from the war zone were effectively shackled, forced to embed with the Russian Army or else fend for themselves in the firestorm. The few brave reporters who chose the second, independent path – Anna Politkovskaia, Andrei Babitsky – were confined to marginal media outlets.

The contrasts between the 1990s and the 2000s may appear more obvious in the realm of economic policy. Where Yeltsin implemented a radical programme of market reforms and mass privatization, seeking to dismantle forever the state socialist system, Putin seemingly moved to expand the state's role. In the Western press, the dismemberment of the oil company Yukos and the incarceration of its oligarch proprietor, Mikhail Khodorkovsky, in 2003 were seen as a major turning point, signs of a creeping renationalization of the economy. By 2004, Putin appointees were in charge of nine companies with assets worth 40 per cent of Russia's GDP – a phenomenon seen as evidence of a turn away from free-market capitalism back toward a statist model.

But this picture, too, changes on closer inspection. Putin's rule has been driven throughout by two parallel impulses, one rooted in neoliberal principles and the other in a strategic statism. Putin's first administration, from 2000 to 2004, was perhaps his most energetically neoliberal, introducing a series of measures designed to extend the reach of private capital: in 2001, a flat income tax set at 13 per cent; in 2002, a labour code scaling back workers' rights; tax cuts for businesses in 2002 and 2003. These moves were widely applauded in the West at the time: the right-wing Heritage Foundation praised 'Russia's flat tax miracle', while Thomas Friedman gushed about Russia's embrace of 'this capitalist thing', urging readers of the *New York Times* to 'keep rootin' for Putin'.[14] His second presidency, too, was marked by moves to increase the private sector's role in education, health and housing, and by the conversion of several in-kind social benefits to cash payments – a 'monetization' that prompted popular protests in the winter of 2004–05, but which was carried through in modified form all the same.

Alongside this liberalizing thrust, however, there was a push by the state to regain control of the 'commanding heights' of the economy. This primarily meant control over natural resources for export, in particular oil and gas. State dominance of the energy sector is not in itself out of the ordinary: majority state ownership is in fact the global norm, and when Putin came to power, Russia was one of very few oil-producing states where production was largely in private hands.[15] Before entering the Kremlin, Putin had expressed a commitment to the idea that the state should play a decisive role in strategic sectors. In 1997, he obtained a doctorate in Russian economic policy and natural resources from the St Petersburg Mining Institute. Chunks of his thesis seem to have been lifted from the work of two US academics, and it's likely Putin didn't write the rest of it either. But its theme was clearly close to his concerns, and a 1999 article on the same subject published under Putin's name argues that the Russian state should assist in the creation of strong, vertically integrated corporations capable of competing with Western firms.[16] Yet even here he insists on a combination of state intervention and market mechanisms. In other words, the statism for which Putin has often been condemned in the Western financial press has always been of a relative, targeted kind.

It's important to bear in mind, too, that the 'statist' component of Putin's economic policies didn't always require actual state ownership. Even as it was handing pieces of Khodorkovsky's Yukos to Rosneft, the Putin government was busy privatizing other major assets: in 2002 it sold off the oil company Slavneft, and in 2004 divested itself of its remaining stake in Lukoil, which went to ConocoPhillips.[17] What's more, even state behemoths like Rosneft and Gazprom are organized like private companies, geared primarily to pay dividends to shareholders – of which the state is simply the largest. There has been little to distinguish the behaviour of many state companies in Russia from that of privately owned ones; the apparent statism of the Putin era is in that sense far removed from the thinking of Soviet economic planners.

This combination of neoliberal and statist impulses produced what the political scientist Gerald Easter calls an 'upstairs-downstairs' economy: large strategic industries remained directly or indirectly subordinated to the state, while private enterprise took care of the rest, from banking and construction to retail and petty trade.[18] But what both strands of Putin's economic policy share is a respect for profit-making. This is not an incidental feature, nor is it simply driven by desires for personal enrichment or corruption at the top. The defining characteristic of the Putin system has been its commitment to defending the capitalist model put in place during the 1990s.

How, then, should the Putin system be described? During the 2000s, a number of terms were applied to it: 'competitive authoritarianism', 'virtual democracy', 'militocracy'.[19] The Kremlin's own ideologues called it 'sovereign democracy' or 'managed democracy' – to which Russian wits responded by saying that either adjective was to 'democracy' what 'electric' is to 'chair'. Later, as Russia's relations with the West began to worsen, new terms joined the latter's lexicon: 'mafia state', 'kleptocracy'.[20] The various labels stressed different aspects of the regime: its increasingly authoritarian bent, reflected in the suppression of dissent and the spread of security service personnel throughout the state apparatus; its hollow performance of democratic rituals such as elections, emptied of any actual democratic content; and its artful manipulation of appearances through its grip on the media. Then there was its endemic corruption, and the entanglement of officialdom with organized crime. All of these features are undoubtedly present in Putin's Russia, and they inflict real damage on the country's socio-economic fabric. But they did not emerge only after 2000: they were present in the 1990s too. Still more crucially, identifying these ills only gets us so far in understanding what the Putin system is. They are symptoms, not causes; they describe the consequences of the system, rather than defining its essence.

Beneath the many labels attached to it, the Putin system is not fundamentally distinct from the one set in place under Yeltsin. It represents, rather, that system's continuation and growth. In his highly astute writings on post-Soviet politics, the late Dmitri Furman argued that we should see Russia's post-Soviet rulers as embodying successive stages in the evolution of a single model: a 'revolutionary' period of destruction of the old regime in the 1990s was followed by one of consolidation in the 2000s.[21] Throughout this period, the dominant political form in the countries of the former USSR was what he termed 'imitation democracy': a system in which a formal commitment to democratic norms and procedures coexisted with a total absence of actual alternatives to the current regime. In most of the Soviet successor states – from Belarus to Kazakhstan, Azerbaijan to Russia – it remained impossible for the opposition to come to power, yet the 'democratic' facade of these regimes required them to hold elections of some kind every few years. This gave rise to recurrent moments of crisis. Indeed, as Furman pointed out, contested votes account for most of the rare occasions when post-Soviet countries broke out of the 'imitation democratic' cycle – Georgia's Rose Revolution of 2003, Ukraine's Orange Revolution of 2004, Kyrgyzstan's Tulip Revolution of 2005. The Russian protests against electoral fraud in late 2011 occurred at another such moment of vulnerability, when the regime's democratic rhetoric ran up against the reality of how it exercised power.

The basic post-Soviet political condition, then, has been one of what Furman called *bezal'ternativnost'* – 'alternativelessness'. Many commentators have located its origins in these countries' supposedly authoritarian political culture, or in some unabashed nostalgia for Stalinism, or in popular distaste for the democratic process. Furman came to rather different conclusions. He held that it developed out of a contradiction that attended the birth of these regimes: the mismatch between the new governments' supposedly democratic goals and the gaping lack of a popular mandate for their programme of free-market transformation.

Every time the requirements of capitalist 'transition' came into conflict with the principle of popular sovereignty, Russia's post-Soviet rulers made it clear enough where their loyalties lay. Yeltsin's attack on the parliament in October 1993 was only the first in a long line of violations designed to shield a nascent post-Soviet capitalism from being held to account by the citizenry. After Yeltsin's re-election in 1996 – secured, it bears repeating, thanks to a combination of electoral fraud and Western meddling – Anatoly Chubais, one of the main architects of privatization in Russia, left the public in no doubt about what had been at stake: 'Russian democracy is irrevocable, private ownership in Russia is irrevocable, market reforms in the Russian state are irrevocable.'[22]

This original contradiction between democratic appearance and capitalist substance was a crack in the foundations of the post-Soviet order, and it was preserved and maintained by Putin after 2000. Rather than overturning the policies of the Yeltsin period, he built on them. There was, however, one important difference between the presidencies of the two men, and it played out in the realm of ideology. Yeltsin, as the dismantler of the Soviet system, could openly embrace the ideology of the free market, as the necessary instrument of the transformation he was pushing through. Putin, though he had come to power as the guarantor of the system's continuity, presented himself as someone who would undo the excesses of the 1990s. His rule was from the outset constitutively riven, defending in practice the outcomes of free-market reforms its rhetoric repudiated, and making nostalgic appeals to a Communist system whose egalitarian principles it rejected.

This contradiction remained the unbreachable limit of the Putin system, preventing it from developing a consistent ideological project. For most of the 2000s, attempts to concoct suitable concepts for it fell flat. 'Sovereign democracy' and 'managed democracy' were more exercises in marketing than expressions of a coherent vision, and didn't gain any traction among the public as a whole. After returning to the Kremlin in 2012 Putin adopted a more stridently nationalistic agenda, in an attempt to give the system a more solid ideological foundation.

The persistence of this dilemma points to the post-Soviet system's conceptual hollowness, its inability to devise an ideological formula to fill the void left by Communism's collapse. Yet despite this weakness, the 'imitation democratic' system commanded first by Yeltsin and then by Putin survived the 1990s and the first decade of the new century intact and largely unchallenged. The reasons for its surprising stability are not to be found in the personal attributes or willpower of whichever man has stood at its summit. They lie instead in the particular forms capitalism has taken in post-Soviet Russia. To understand that, we need to look more closely at the distinctive relationship between money and power that emerged in the 1990s, and at the changing character of the society over which Yeltsin and Putin have presided.

CHAPTER 2

Faces of Power

I N THE SPRING OF 2014, the US, the EU, Canada and several
other countries imposed sanctions on dozens of individuals,
many of them high-ranking friends of Putin, in response to
Russia's annexation of Crimea. These sanctions have been extended
and renewed several times, most dramatically in the spring of
2018, after the attempted killing of a former Russian spy in the
UK produced yet another diplomatic crisis between Russia and
the West. Sanctions, it seems, have all but become a permanent
feature of Western policy towards Russia: in 2017 the US Congress
enshrined them in law, and although some European governments
have occasionally made noises about revisiting the question, they,
too, remain committed to sanctions for now.

The West has repeatedly used sanctions to try to force trouble-
some states into line – with limited success. The sanctions on Russia,
like those applied to other countries, are rooted in the notion that
punishing a select circle of people at the top is tantamount to disci-
plining the country as a whole. The individuals targeted after 2014,
for example, included the Russian and Ukrainian officials who
played an active role in the annexation – from high-level Kremlin
operators such as Igor Sechin, a close ally of Putin, and Vladislav

Surkov, the Machiavellian inventor of the term 'managed democracy', to the men charged with implementing Moscow's policy on the ground in Crimea. But the sanctions list also included many private businessmen deemed to be close to the Kremlin. There were Yuri Kovalchuk and Nikolai Shamalov, the two largest single shareholders in Bank Rossiia, widely rumoured to operate as a private bank for senior Russian officials. And there were individuals known to have personal connections with Putin – and to have profited handsomely from them – such as Gennady Timchenko, whose firm, Gunvor, rapidly grew from almost nothing in 2000 to become the third-largest oil trader in the world by 2007. There were also the Rotenberg brothers, Arkady and Boris, whose construction firm won $7 billion worth of no-bid contracts for the 2014 Winter Olympics in Sochi.[1] The 2018 US sanctions focused still more closely on Putin's inner circle, targeting his son-in-law Kirill Shamalov, as well as businessmen linked to the Kremlin such as Vladimir Bogdanov and Oleg Deripaska.

According to the logic of the sanctions, since power and wealth are highly concentrated in Russia, punishing those with personal connections to Putin is the best way to strike at the heart of the regime. Yet the belief that a handful of people wield absolute political and economic power over the country – or that it is ruled by a 'kleptocracy' centred on Putin[2] – mistakes a symptom for a prime cause. Even if sanctions brought about a change in policy or personnel, they would do little to alter the underlying conditions that produced the regime in the first place. As suggested in the last chapter, the Putin system isn't simply a corrupt, dictatorial structure imposed on a helpless population; it's embedded in the social, economic and political fabric of the country. In other words, if we really want to understand how Russia is ruled, we need to look beyond the individuals at the summits of wealth and power to the system that enables them to thrive.

Behind the question of who runs and owns Russia lies another, larger question: what kind of capitalism has taken root there since the fall of the USSR? Just as the conventional wisdom draws a sharp distinction between the chaotic but broadly liberal political system of the 1990s and the creeping authoritarianism of the 2000s, there is a tendency to depict the Yeltsin era as representing the advance of the free market, and the Putin years as a retreat back into statism. For some observers, by the mid-2000s Russia was well on its way to becoming a 'corporate state' – dubbed Kremlin, Inc., since its main shareholders seemed to be largely concentrated within the medieval fortress in the capital's heart; or else KGB, Inc., for those who felt the security services were running the show.[3] The Western financial press in particular saw the apparent extension of state control as an attempt to reverse the 1990s market reforms. By 2007 Anders Åslund, a former adviser to the Yeltsin government, was bemoaning the fact that Putin had 'unleashed a great wave of renationalization', adding that the president's 'chums from St Petersburg are taking over one big, well-run private company after another, turning them into less efficient state-owned firms'.[4] This was no longer the familiar liberal capitalism of the 1990s, but an ugly hybrid of the Soviet planned economy and something older – 'state capitalism', 'crony capitalism', 'neo-feudal capitalism'.[5]

This view, though dominant, is misguided. It is based on a fundamental misreading of the relationship between the state and private capital in post-Soviet times. It assumes, in particular, that state and business are distinct realms, and that business has since 2000 been struggling to protect its legitimate terrain of activity from the clutches of an overbearing state. The standout example usually offered of this is the dismantling of Mikhail Khodorkovsky's oil company, Yukos, and the passage of its fragments into state hands after 2003. But in fact the domains of state and business are closely intertwined, and have been since the fall of the USSR.

The best way to understand this is to look at the Russian elite – in particular, at its emergence at the end of the Soviet period, and its subsequent mutations. The story most often told is that the oligarchs of the 1990s piled up their fortunes through the rough-and-tumble of private initiative, whereas the magnates created under Putin derived theirs solely from proximity to the Kremlin. Yet the oligarchs of the Yeltsin era were always closely entangled with the state, and from the outset owed their fortunes to it. The cronyism attributed to the Putin years was central to the making of Russian capitalism long before Putin took the stage.

The history of post-Soviet capitalism should be understood not as a lurch away from free markets toward statism, but as a series of struggles for power and profit within a single elite that spanned the worlds of government and private business. The symbiotic entwinement of the two domains accounts for many of the Putin system's most distinctive characteristics: the strength of its grip on power and profits, but also the corruption and illegality that have done so much to undermine its domestic and international legitimacy. Often ascribed to the rapaciousness and ruthless ambition of individuals, these phenomena are also enabled by the particular form capitalism has taken in Russia.

The symbiosis of state and business that defines Russian capitalism today has its origins in the late Soviet period, when the relationship between political and economic power began to change. For most of the USSR's history, it was not material wealth that defined the ruling elite, but an individual's position within the party–state apparatus. The *nomenklatura*, the core of the administrative elite, enjoyed privileges denied to the mass of the population: spacious apartments, holiday homes, even chauffeurs and servants, as well as access to special shops stocking scarce goods. Party membership, too, conferred advantages, especially in terms of career advancement or favours that could be called in through informal channels. Economic status was firmly subordinated to political power. But in the final Soviet years, the ground started to shift.

The first seeds of a new economic elite were planted in the late 1980s, as Gorbachev's reforms started to open up possibilities for private enrichment. For a few entrepreneurs, arbitrage was one way to make lucrative gains in these years. The state monopoly on foreign trade was abolished in 1986, but internal price controls were not, so for a time, huge profits could be made by exploiting the difference between domestic and export prices. Boris Berezovsky, then a mathematician at the Institute of Control Sciences, did especially well out of such trade, buying computers and cars at subsidized rates and then reselling them. Others of the future oligarchs of the 1990s – Aleksandr Smolensky, Vladimir Gusinsky – began to pull in tidy sums from currency speculation, betting on fluctuations in the rouble exchange rate.

Another kind of financial alchemy provided the basis for Mikhail Khodorkovsky's fortune. As deputy head of the Communist Youth League (Komsomol) at his university, he was well placed to take advantage of the tax breaks and subsidies the organization was granted by the government – along with an almost magical monetary power. The Soviet economy used two forms of money, 'cash' and 'non-cash' roubles; the former were mainly used to pay wages, while the latter were a planning and accounting device, used to allocate resources across the entire economy – hence there were generally far more of them. 'Cash' and 'non-cash' accounts were kept strictly separate – until the end of 1987, when the Komsomol was granted permission to convert non-cash budgetary allocations into actual currency. According to Olga Kryshtanovskaia, the leading Russian expert on the Soviet and post-Soviet elites, Khodorkovsky realized he had found a way of 'making money out of thin air', and quickly set up his own bank.[6]

At first, Russia's most successful entrepreneurs were those who exploited the cracks that were appearing in the planned economy. But soon enough, state enterprise managers and *apparatchiks* were joining the fray. In May 1988, the Supreme Soviet passed the law

'On Cooperation', which allowed groups of individuals to establish self-financed, self-managing cooperatives. The cooperative sector rapidly mushroomed: by 1989 there were 193,000 of them, employing a workforce of 5 million and accounting for more than 4 per cent of GDP.[7] Billed as the spearhead of a new, competitive market economy, cooperatives were in practice mostly attached, barnacle-like, to the old system. The vast majority were closely connected with state-owned enterprises. Often they were simply a way to siphon money into a few select hands: the 'members' who received dividends tended to be the managers of an enterprise rather than its workforce. Cooperatives were also allowed to set up their own financial arms, producing a plethora of 'pocket banks' that could borrow from the central bank at low rates – and of course issue 'loans' to members.

In 1989, managerial personnel and figures from the state apparatus began directly appropriating pieces of the planned economy. This was the beginning of what is called latent privatization.[8] Local bosses turned factories into joint-stock companies in which they awarded themselves majority stakes. Meanwhile, regional officials used Party funds to set up banks and firms where they would then take up cosy executive positions.

The party–state apparatus was also rushing into business: the Communist Party set up commercial banks and hard-currency hotels, while the KGB developed similar business interests of its own. At the same time, entire blocs of the Soviet economy were being taken out of ministerial control and placed under that of new commercial entities. In 1989, the natural gas ministry became the company Gazprom, and the same year the ministry of metallurgy spawned the firm Norilsk Nickel, while the state bodies responsible for water, construction, chemicals and petroleum refining had morphed into dozens upon dozens of new firms. Most of these were still 'state-owned', but did not remain so for long.

At this stage, then, there were two main pools of recruits for the emergent economic elite: entrepreneurs, who capitalized on the

Soviet state's disintegration, and Party *apparatchiks* and industrial managers, who increasingly seized assets under their purview. Common to both groups was the essentially parasitic nature of their fortunes. Much would change during the upheavals of the 1990s, but the foundational dependence of economic wealth on political power would not be undone.

The disappearance of the USSR in 1991 was followed by one of the most dramatic transfers of property in history. Brash new private fortunes were made, giving rise to a layer of oligarchs who came to dominate the headlines. The likes of Berezovsky, Smolensky, Gusinsky and Khodorkovsky looked to be the new power in the land. For many Russians, the sudden arrival of these *nouveaux riches* demonstrated the ascendancy of private wealth over state authority. Yet their wealth was essentially created by the largesse of the country's political rulers.

Nothing demonstrates this more clearly than the process of privatization – widely referred to at the time as *prikhvatizatsiia*, 'grab-it-ization'. The Yeltsin government's massive sell-off of state assets was explicitly designed to smash the Soviet command economy and create a market system dominated by a new class of wealth-holders. Anatoly Chubais, head of the State Property Committee, told one interviewer that 'every enterprise ripped out of the state and transferred to the hands of a private owner was a way of destroying Communism in Russia . . . At that stage, it didn't matter at all to whom these enterprises went, who was getting the property.' The huge imbalances of wealth, power and opportunity this created were just something the populace would have to accept: in November 1992, Chubais shrugged that 'if the problem is only that the rich will buy up the property, I am sure that is the way it must be.'[9]

Privatization took three forms, each of which benefited different segments of the nascent economic elite.[10] The first was a 'mass privatization' scheme, launched with great fanfare in October 1992, in which citizens were issued with vouchers entitling them to buy shares in enterprises slated for privatization. By June 1994, some 15,000 enterprises, employing 17 million people – around two-thirds of the industrial workforce – had been auctioned off.[11] Nominally intended to create a kind of 'popular capitalism', in practice this produced a concentration of ownership and control among well-placed insiders from the *nomenklatura* and Soviet managerial elite. Managers often gained control of their workers' shares, either by purchasing them or through more underhand means. And because voucher privatization took place in the middle of a catastrophic downturn, many workers sold their vouchers at a fraction of their face value to get hold of desperately needed cash. There was also a rash of speculation: by mid-1994, 'voucher funds' had hoovered up almost a third of all the vouchers in the country.[12]

The crisis conditions had another crucial effect: the assessed value of state enterprises was not indexed to inflation, so the real cost of acquiring them was plummeting by the day. The result was a fire sale of the Soviet economic apparatus. The voucher-auction price of shares in Gazprom, the Soviet gas monopoly, implied the company's total value was $228 million – about one-thousandth of the estimation made by Western investment banks at the time. All told, the total value of Russian industry, according to voucher auction prices, was a mere $12 billion. As the *Washington Post's* former Moscow bureau chief David Hoffman put it, this meant that 'the equity of all Russian factories, including oil, gas, some transportation, and most of manufacturing, was worth less than that of Kellogg or Anheuser-Busch'.[13]

The second main form privatization took was even less transparent, involved much larger sums of money, and transferred far more significant assets out of state hands. Starting in mid-1992, Yeltsin effectively created a pool of magnates by state fiat, through a process of 'privatization by decree' that kept transactions free from democratic scrutiny. This involved, in particular, the enormous assets of the natural resource sector – oil and gas, coal, diamonds, gold, and so on. The new owners were initially drawn mostly from among the 'red directors' who had managed these concerns under Soviet rule. Among the enterprises sold off or turned into joint-stock companies by executive order were Gazprom; Rosugol, the state coal concern; Alrosa, a diamond company; and, crucially, three giant oil companies – Yukos, Lukoil, and Surgutneftegaz.[14] Again, the prices these assets fetched were light-years from any market valuation; the Yeltsin government's eagerness to shift chunks of the economy into private hands took precedence over rational economic calculations.

A third form of privatization involved not state assets but budgetary flows. After 1991, Komsomol entrepreneurs such as Khodorkovsky and canny operators like Berezovsky or Smolensky acquired formidable power and wealth by acting as 'authorized' intermediaries for a range of government bodies. Funds for many of the ministries were not handled by the central bank, but instead routed through accounts in various privately owned 'plenipotentiary' banks. Like the winners of the voucher auctions and the magnates designated by decree, the new financial tycoons were effectively subsidized by the state. They even admitted as much: Khodorkovsky confessed to one interviewer that his Menatep Bank was deliberately organized to mirror the structure of the government, the better to maintain its grasp on federal revenues. As another banker, Pyotr Aven, observed:

> To become a millionaire in our country, it is not at all necessary to have a good head or specialized knowledge. Often it is enough to have active support in the government, the parliament, local power structures and law enforcement agencies. One fine day, your insignificant bank is authorized to, for instance, conduct operations with budgetary funds. Or quotas are generously allotted for the export of oil, timber and gas. In other words, you are appointed a millionaire.[15]

Similar processes were taking place at the regional level, though the pace and scale varied. In Moscow, Mayor Yuri Luzhkov governed in the manner of an old-school Party boss from 1992 to 2010. Instead of selling off their massive portfolio of properties, the municipal authorities kept hold of them, and retained a far greater degree of financial autonomy than any other Russian region. Here private fortunes were made mainly through lucrative city contracts secured thanks to connections with the mayor's office, notably in construction – Luzhkov's wife, Elena Baturina, head of the building firm Inteko, was coincidentally among the tiny number of women to join the hyper-rich.

Across the other eighty-odd federal components of Russia, the picture was complicated: while some local elites enthusiastically embraced free-market reforms, others created personal fiefdoms, sometimes on a clan or ethnic basis. But overall, the peripheries echoed what was happening in the Kremlin: in one region after another, the governor served as 'midwife to the creation of financial-industrial groups' – as political scientist Thomas Remington described it – forming a local elite by means of privatization.[16]

Who were the men – and they were almost without exception men – who made up Russia's new elite in the 1990s? In an impressive 2009 statistical study, economist Serguey Braguinsky profiled nearly 300 of its members.[17] He divided them into two categories that to some extent reflected the pools from which the embryonic elite of the late 1980s was drawn – the canny operators versus the *apparatchiks*. Almost half of Braguinsky's sample – 45 per cent – were what he called 'insiders': managers of Soviet enterprises prior to 1991, members of the *nomenklatura*, and relatives or close colleagues of people in the first two groups. The slight majority, by contrast, were classed as 'outsiders', with no visibly important ties to the previous system. The people in these two categories had quite different demographic and social profiles. The majority of 'insiders' were from the provinces (66 per cent), and overwhelmingly Slavic in origin (85 per cent); by contrast, two-fifths of 'outsiders' were born in Moscow, and a quarter were Jewish.* (Part of the reason for this disproportion is that in the late Soviet period Jews had faced a good deal of discrimination, and were hence much less likely to be appointed to 'insider' managerial posts.)

This distinction between 'insiders' and 'outsiders' is especially significant because it sheds light on the murky battles over power and property that were then unfolding. Often depicted as a simple struggle between oligarch-entrepreneurs and the vestiges of the planned economy, between business and the state, these battles should more properly be understood as fluctuations in the relative influence of the two categories of tycoon. Both 'insiders' and 'outsiders' profited from the different forms of privatization – 'red directors' seizing the factories under their control, entrepreneurs setting up banks, ex-Komsomol members and oilmen acquiring mines and wells by decree. But there were also some crucial differences between the two groups, and these help us understand what did and did not change in Russian capitalism from the 1990s to the 2000s.

One was the broad sectoral division that emerged. 'Insiders' dominated large-scale industry – natural resources, energy, metallurgy, engineering – while 'outsiders' mostly made their initial fortunes in banking, consumer goods, the media. One group tended to own physical assets, the other financial wealth. For much of the 1990s, economic conditions favoured the 'outsiders': industrial production was crippled, and those with access to large

---

* In Russia, Jewishness is generally held to be an ethnic category, and is often registered in official census data along with other *narodnosti* – 'nationalities' – such as Tatars, Chechens, Buryats, and so on. The share of the Russian population identifying as Jews in 2002, in the first post-Soviet census, was 0.16 per cent.

reserves of cash had the edge.* By the middle of the decade, 'outsider' oligarchs had used this advantage to extend their holdings into other sectors, grabbing assets ranging from mines to airlines, factories to TV stations. Berezovsky, for instance, came to own Aeroflot, the car giant Avtovaz, the public TV station ORT and the newspaper *Nezavisimaia gazeta*. Gusinsky's holdings included Most-Bank, the television station NTV and newspapers such as *Segodnia*. Smolensky owned Agroprombank and the newspaper *Kommersant*. Mikhail Fridman and Pyotr Aven jointly dominated Alfa-Bank.

A second key difference lay in the two groups' attitudes toward the state. These were rooted in fundamentally divergent experiences. Insiders, as their name suggests, tended to be better connected to the regional and national government apparatus, often through informal ties forged in the Soviet era. These now served as a form of political insurance, allowing them to secure state approval or assistance for their business activities. Outsiders, on the other hand, had largely profited from symptoms of the USSR's collapse, and lacked such connections. As a result, they had to seek insurance in other ways: either through bribery or by funding their own candidates for political office. During the course of the 1990s, when 'outsiders' had the advantage economically, they were also more active than 'insiders' in pressing forward their interests politically. The penetration of state institutions by business interests was especially marked in the Duma: according to one astute analyst, in the 1990s 'most deputies were more or less openly on the payroll of one oligarch or another.'[18]

By the mid-1990s, it had begun to seem as if the 'outsiders' had gained the upper hand not only over the 'insiders', but also over the state itself. Perhaps the most flagrant demonstration of this came

---

* Of course, 'insiders' could still make money from their industrial holdings through transfer pricing, creative accounting or asset-stripping; but it was much more difficult to turn a profit from production itself.

in late 1995, with the infamous 'loans-for-shares' deals. Strapped for cash and in desperate need of support for his re-election bid the following year, Yeltsin authorized a series of rigged auctions through which stakes in a dozen companies were offered to select oligarchs as collateral on loans totalling $1 billion. In exchange, the media outlets they owned offered full-throated backing for Yeltsin's presidential campaign. When the auctions went ahead in November–December 1995, rival bidders were excluded, in some cases physically: local authorities in the Siberian town of Surgut ordered the airport to be closed while the oil company Surgutneftegaz sold a 40 per cent stake to its own pension fund.

The biggest winners, inevitably, were the most powerful billionaires. Vladimir Potanin, who had come up with the scheme in the first place, paid just $170 million for Norilsk Nickel, a company with revenues of $3.3 billion and profits of $1.2 billion in 1995. He and his associate Mikhail Prokhorov also picked up a majority stake in the oil company Sidanco for $130 million. Khodorkovsky acquired 78 per cent of the oil company Yukos for $300 million; within two years it would have a market capitalization of $9 billion.[19] Another oil company, Sibneft, went to Berezovsky for just $100 million; a few years later it had a market capitalization of $1 billion.[20]

'Loans for shares' is often invoked as the most brazenly crooked of the Yeltsin government's privatizations, which it probably was. But it was not, as is commonly supposed, the origin of the leading oligarchs' wealth. Rather, it stood as public proof of these outsider tycoons' hold on the country, and of their ability to bend the state to their will. Having acquired phenomenal wealth during the first half of the decade, they now used it to obtain political power, the better to cement their grip on their fortunes. After all, they had so far made their money between the cracks of the state; how much more could they make if they were in control of the whole thing? Sure enough, once Yeltsin was safely reinstalled in the Kremlin in the summer of 1996, the oligarchs began to arrange a further carve-up of state assets. In 1997, for example, a bitter feud erupted among them over telecoms provider Sviazinvest. That year, when American diplomat Thomas Graham asked an unnamed oligarch if it wasn't time to start investing in production, he replied, 'No . . . we still have to divide up all the property.' Since Russia was a big country, he added, this would take some time.[21]

In January 1996, just after the loans-for-shares auctions, sociologist Olga Kryshtanovskaia was among the first to popularize a new term for Russia's elite: she argued that the country was witnessing the emergence of a new 'oligarchy', since the biggest tycoons not only dominated the national economy, they were also beginning to control the political scene.[22] Berezovsky – appointed deputy head of the National Security Council that October – famously boasted that he and the other oligarchs owned half the economy; it began to seem as if they had privatized the government too. 'From my point of view,' Berezovsky told one interviewer, 'in general, power and capital are inseparable'. He added, after a pause, that 'if something is advantageous to capital, it goes without saying that it is advantageous to the nation'.[23] Wealth seemed to be dictating terms to power, in a phenomenon often referred to as state capture.

But this apparent victory for capital over the state was deceptive, in two respects. Firstly, it was not so much a triumph of private business as of a specific kind of businessman – the 'outsider'. The outsiders' ascendancy was based on years of success in exploiting a combination of government largesse and disarray in the state apparatus, and on the persistence of an economic depression that placed the 'insiders' at a disadvantage. But, secondly, despite what the outsider oligarchs and many others seemed to think at the time, neither of these conditions was permanent. What looked like 'state capture' was not a definitive seizure of political power by the economic elite as a whole, but a temporary surge in the influence of one of its factions. For most of the 1990s, the pendulum had swung toward the outsiders; soon, both of the preconditions for their dominance would vanish, and it would start to swing the other way.

The new century seemed to bring an abrupt break with the oligarch-dominated politics of the 1990s. Early in his presidency, in July 2000, Putin met with twenty-one of the country's richest tycoons and reportedly spelled out new rules of the game: the state would now remain 'equidistant' from all business interests, and the latter would refrain from attempting to direct state policy. Those who abided by these rules could continue to enjoy their fortunes; those who did not, it soon became clear, would be expropriated and hounded out of the country. Gusinsky, whose media empire had been critical of Putin during the 1999–2000 election cycle, was forced to sell his prize assets and flee to Spain. Berezovsky, who had boasted of his role as Kremlin kingmaker in bringing Putin to power, soon followed: he quickly lost control of ORT, Russia's main TV channel, and by November 2000 was in exile in the UK.

The anti-oligarchic turn seemed to gather pace dramatically in October 2003, when Russia's wealthiest man stepped from his private jet onto the tarmac of Novosibirsk's Tolmachevo airport, only to be handcuffed by a group of armed FSB men in black fatigues. Khodorkovsky spent the next ten years in prison, ostensibly for tax fraud, while his oil company, Yukos, was dismembered and then mostly absorbed by the state-owned Rosneft. The case sent tremors through the ranks of the Russian oligarchy: if Khodorkovsky's assets could be seized, no one else was safe. It also prompted outrage in Western capitals and financial centres, which saw it as the first ominous sign of a coming re-nationalization of the Russian economy.

More portents of the same kind followed, from state acquisition of assets to a rise in the number of state representatives on the boards of private companies. Between 2003 and 2007, for instance, the Russian state went from owning the equivalent of 20 per cent of the country's stock market capitalization to owning 35 per cent, and by 2006, according to the *Financial Times*, '11 members [of the Putin administration] chaired 6 state companies and had 12 further state directorships; 15 senior government officials held 6 chairmanships and 24 other board seats.'[24] If what had taken place under Yeltsin was 'state capture' – oligarchs effectively privatizing large chunks of the government apparatus – in the 2000s the boot seemed to be on the other foot, as the state laid claim to swathes of private enterprise; in effect, 'business capture'.[25]

Yet behind this apparent encroachment of the state into business, there was no fundamental turn against the principle of private profit. What changed under Putin were the sources of wealth, the identity of its individual holders, and the methods used to maintain and extend it. To begin with, for all the anti-oligarchic talk, there was no let-up in the creation of immense personal fortunes. Indeed, although Putin publicly promised that the oligarchs would 'cease to exist as a class' – a phrase with unmistakable echoes of the judgement Stalin had passed on the *kulaks* – the number of billionaires in Russia, according to *Forbes*, went from zero in 2000 to eighty-two in early 2008, on the eve of the global economic crisis. The downturn that followed trimmed their numbers somewhat, to fifty-seven in 2010, but by 2017 – even after several years of slow or negative growth and sanctions from the West – Russia had ninety-six billionaires. Over all this time, brazen displays of wealth multiplied, as Russian oligarchs lavished money on English football clubs, mega-yachts and palatial pieces of real estate. To the west of Moscow in particular, an area considered an elite enclave during Soviet times, the construction of opulent mansions and gated compounds carved more and more flashy holes in the forest.

The expanding ranks of the super-wealthy featured many new faces, and the fortunes of the Putin-era billionaires were based in different sectors of the economy from those of the Yeltsin years. This shift mostly took place after 2000, but its real origins lie in the rouble crash and debt default of 1998. The crash meant, first of all, that the advantage previously enjoyed by those with financial wealth began to evaporate. Smolensky's SBS Agro Bank failed, while Potanin and Berezovsky were forced to dispose of assets. (Chubais did, though, think to let the oligarchs know in advance about the default, allowing them to spirit some of their cash overseas before the rouble lost a quarter of its value.)[26]

At the same time, the currency devaluation boosted Russian domestic production by making imports more expensive, strengthening oligarchs with assets in manufacturing, agriculture, food processing and distribution, and so on. A new bankruptcy law passed a few months before the rouble crisis also proved significant in its wake: companies were allowed to seize assets in payment of debts, prompting a rash of bankruptcy suits and an accelerating debt roll-up.[27] And in reducing the weight of Moscow-based financiers, the 1998 crash had an immediate geographical effect: a number of regional 'financial-industrial groups' formed in the mid-1990s weathered the storm better than many national-level concerns.

The surge in raw materials prices after 1999 hugely accelerated the reshaping of the Russian elite that began with the rouble crash. In 1997, only a few of the top ten oligarchs had interests outside banking or the media. After the turn of the century, almost all of the top ten owed their wealth to metals or mineral resources. A handful of players from the 1990s remained, but they tended to be precisely those with holdings in the newly buoyant sectors: aluminium magnate Oleg Deripaska, banker-turned-nickel baron Vladimir Potanin, metals and oil tycoon Roman Abramovich. Meanwhile, banking and media figures such as Berezovsky and Gusinsky were replaced in the 2000s by the likes of Aleksei Mordashov, owner of steelmaker Severstal; Vladimir Lisin, head of the Novolipetsk steel combine; and Mikhail Prokhorov, co-owner with Potanin of Norilsk Nickel.

Along with these sectoral shifts came changes in the social and demographic profile of the business elite, and a recalibration of the balance between 'insiders' and 'outsiders'. As industrial and extractive concerns became more prominent in the 2000s, the predominance of Moscow decreased and the influence of industrial and resource-rich regions such as the Urals and Western Siberia rose. By 2007, only seven of the top forty oligarchs came from Moscow; most of the rest were from cities or smaller towns in the country's vast hinterland. This signified a tilt, too, in favour of 'insiders': as domestic industry revived and natural-resource prices rocketed, the assets that had been seized a decade earlier by former factory managers, 'red directors' and members of the old *apparat* became highly lucrative, bumping their owners much further up the rich list.

At the same time, the weight and role of the state in private profit-making also underwent a mutation. But this did not happen because of a statist takeover or 'business capture'. Instead, 'insiders' and, increasingly, state functionaries themselves turned the apparatus of the state – no longer in such disarray as it had been in the 1990s – into an instrument for private profit. That is, they were doing what the 'outsiders' had done in the 1990s, but from a different starting position: close to or inside the state. In fact, one of the striking things about the apparent 'statist' turn of the 2000s was the degree to which participants replicated the modus operandi of private companies in the 1990s. State-owned companies used the tax-avoidance strategies pioneered by the oligarchs, parking shares in offshore companies or routing transactions through intermediaries. Once again, this was accompanied by corrupt privatizations, asset-stripping, and threats of violence. In 2002, for example, there was a period when the state-owned oil company Slavneft had two chief executives, each equipped with a court order and a small private army.[28]

The Yukos affair was perhaps the starkest example of how standard business practices of the 1990s seeped into the state sector in the 2000s. The seizure and dismantling of the company was not so much a forcible re-nationalization as a colossal state-directed piece of *reiderstvo*, the post-Soviet version of corporate raiding. Assets were acquired cheaply by coercive means, with raiders often making physical threats to force the transfer of shares, or else bribing a bureaucrat to issue a court order or start bankruptcy proceedings. They were then resold at a huge profit. The use of state resources was central to these operations. In the 1990s, it was the raiders who bribed the state. Under Putin, state functionaries themselves seized companies, hiring raiders to act on their behalf.

Many explanations for the fate of Yukos have been advanced: Khodorkovsky's attempts to sell a stake to the US oil major Chevron; his plans to build a private pipeline to China, competing with the state's line to Japan; his support for opposition parties and apparent desire to run for president in 2008; the personal disrespect he is alleged to have shown to Putin. All of these likely contributed to his downfall.[29] But more than anything, his ruin was intended as a raw demonstration of state power, and to lay out a new elite bargain in which those with links to state power had the upper hand over those who simply had money. Yukos was one of several companies put under pressure by the tax authorities during 2003; others included Norilsk Nickel, Sibneft and Vimpelcom. Within weeks of Khodorkovsky's arrest, the Federal Assembly's Accounts Chamber announced it was 'revisiting' the outcomes of the 1990s privatizations, while Putin and other officials made statements to the effect that business needed to show 'social responsibility', 'assisting' the state in its 'priority tasks'.

This did not mean, however, that those now pressing home their advantage were advancing the interests of the state, let alone those of the public. State companies pursued what were effectively private agendas. During the 2000s, for example, Russia's state-owned enterprises went on a buying spree, loading themselves with debt in order to acquire more and more assets, not in pursuit of national policy goals but to increase the value of their stocks.[30]

As OECD economist William Tompson put it, although the state sector did indeed act independently of big business, 'it did not necessarily act differently'.[31]

There was, then, an increasing convergence in the logic and practices of the state and private sectors of the economy. This phenomenon was rooted in the close entanglement of business and government over the whole post-Soviet era. While this initially took the form of a parasitic dependency of business on the state, by the mid-1990s the business elite had begun to penetrate the state and indeed aspire to control it. The reassertion of state authority after 2000, and increased hydrocarbon revenues, changed the terms of the equation. But what took place under Putin was not simply a push in the opposite direction from the 1990s. Rather, there was a synthesis of the realms of government and business – the features of one merging with those of the other. This melding of state and business spheres accounts for many of the most damaging aspects of the way Russia is ruled today; it also means that we need to think differently about who is doing the ruling.

Over the course of the 2000s, a widespread consensus developed that Putin had set in place a 'neo-KGB state', a 'praetorian regime run by people from the secret services' whose authoritarian instincts explained the darkening prospects for democracy and free speech in Russia.[32] After all, Putin himself had come from the ranks of the KGB, and he steadily recruited more men from the security services into his government. The *siloviki*, as they were known – after the 'power structures', *silovye struktury*, from which they originated – included some of Putin's closest allies: Igor Sechin, chairman of Rosneft; Sergei Ivanov, defence minister from 2001 to 2007 and later Putin's chief of staff; and Viktor Ivanov, who from 2008 to 2016 was head of the FSKN, the federal anti-drug agency. But there were many more, all the way down the chain of command.

The empirical basis for the idea of a creeping *silovik* takeover came from Olga Kryshtanovskaia and Stephen White, who in a series of influential articles characterized Putin's rule as a 'militocracy'. In 2003, they calculated that across several key sectors of government, the proportion of current and former security service personnel had risen sharply from the Yeltsin era, accounting for a quarter of the political elite; in 2009, they argued that the proportion had increased to almost one-third.[33]

The idea seemed plausible, especially given Putin's own background and the macho security-service language that set the tone for much of his time in office. It certainly resonated strongly far beyond academic and policymaking circles, both in Russia and in the West. For two Russian journalists, Andrei Soldatov and Irina Borogan, this cluster of uniforms constituted a 'new nobility'. In a grim satire set in 2028, Vladimir Sorokin, *enfant terrible* of Russian literature, reimagined them as a deeper throwback, to the *oprichnina*, Ivan the Terrible's private army, which terrorized Muscovy in the late sixteenth century.[34] In another phantasmagorical satire on post-Soviet reality, novelist Viktor Pelevin took a trope in wide circulation at the time, the 'werewolf in epaulets', and made it literal, depicting Russia's current rulers as petroleum-worshipping beasts in KGB attire, howling at the earth to deliver the bounty on which their power depended.[35]

But the term 'militocracy' is misleading for several reasons. One is that the apparent rise of the *siloviki* predates Putin. To take only the obvious examples, among the Yeltsin-era appointees with a KGB background were Aleksandr Korzhakov, the president's bodyguard, as well as three successive prime ministers – Evgeny Primakov, Sergei Stepashin and, of course, Putin himself. Second, the category of *silovik* itself is too broad. As used by Kryshtanovskaia and White, it tends to conflate actual military personnel with, say, clerical staff working at a 'power ministry'. It also makes no allowance for the nature or duration of service: statistically, an employee of six months' standing in the PR department of the Emergencies

Ministry is as much a *silovik* as a KGB general with several decades of experience.[36]

More importantly, however, the focus on the *siloviki* draws attention away from other, equally significant changes in the configuration of the elite. As Kryshtanovskaia and White themselves record, between 1993 and 2003 'representatives of big business' came to account for an increasing share of the country's political leadership – rising from zero to one-fifth of government ministers.[37] By the end of the century, two successive ministers of fuel and energy had been recruited from oil companies, and a whole section of Putin's early appointments to the presidential administration came directly from Alfa-Bank.

The same trend applied at the regional level: in the 1990s, only a few businessmen had been heads of federal subunits, but after 2000, examples multiplied, starting with Roman Abramovich taking on the governorship of frozen Chukotka, the country's easternmost region. By 2002, almost a third of the Federation Council – the legislature's upper house, comprising representatives from all of Russia's federal components – had come from private enterprise.[38] Sometimes the head of a region was also the executive of its largest company, as in the case of Aleksandr Khloponin, chairman of Norilsk Nickel, who ran Krasnoyarsk region from 2002 to 2010. As Kryshtanovskaia and White themselves observed in 2009, 'the tendency for regional capital and government to merge has become increasingly powerful': representatives of financial-industrial groups were moving into elected office in the towns, while state-farm managers came to dominate the countryside.[39]

At the same time, while many figures from business were shifting into the sphere of government, there was also a good deal of movement in the other direction: businesses were recruiting from the ranks of government ministries. In the 1990s, a large part of the post-Soviet business elite was drawn from among the *nomenklatura* and 'red directors'. The difference now was that figures leaving the state apparatus were doing so to join existing business concerns rather than set up new ones. By 2001, an estimated fifth of the business elite had previously been state officials.[40]

This two-way traffic between the worlds of the state and of private enterprise will no doubt be entirely familiar to many readers: the same kind of revolving door notoriously sustains elites around much of the globe, enabling them to waltz effortlessly between the boardrooms of Goldman Sachs and the corridors of power in Washington, London, Rome and elsewhere. Russia's government and business became similarly interwoven, leading to the emergence of an increasingly hybrid elite, able to hop amphibiously between domains that were formally separate but which for them, in practice, were one. In 2007, after an internal tussle between different security services burst into the open,* the then head of the anti-drug agency, Viktor Cherkesov, published an article titled 'We Should Not Allow Warriors to Turn into Traders'.[41] Ostensibly a principled plea to keep business and state service separate, Cherkesov's unusually public intervention was disingenuous in the extreme: its real purpose was to call a truce between arms of the state that were already at odds over their business interests. 'Traders' and 'warriors', and indeed businessmen and statesmen more generally, had long since become indistinguishable categories.

The increasingly close overlap between the realms of state and business had severe consequences for the rest of the population. It meant above all that the elite could deploy the formal power of the state for personal ends. State functionaries used entirely legal means – tax inspections, bankruptcy laws and property transfer

---

* FSB agents had arrested a high-level officer of the FSKN in connection with a bribery investigation; the arrested man countered by accusing top FSB agents of involvement in a smuggling and tax-evasion scheme, which he had apparently been investigating.

documents – to gain control of companies, banks, oil fields. (The Russian elite can be intensely legalistic in its felonies, in the spirit of the proverb: 'For our friends we have everything; for our enemies, the law.')

As policymaking and the pursuit of profit bled into one another, a range of malign symptoms began to manifest themselves across Russian society. In addition to practising *reiderstvo* on businesses and on each other, state functionaries at all levels squeezed the populace for cash. The sums involved ranged from the relatively minor amounts demanded by traffic cops to the levies of $1,000 per month 'lifted' from small businesses by government agencies. As for high-end political corruption, in the mid-2000s, amendments to existing legislation cost $200,000; for $500,000 you could get your own law custom-made; a false budget entry cost 4 per cent of the sum involved.[42] Informally, it came to be understood that certain state personnel would 'look after' specific sectors or companies, which became known as *poliany*, 'grazing grounds'. The echo of the early modern Muscovite institution of *kormlenie*, 'feeding', which licensed nobles to enrich themselves at the expense of designated territories, was one reason why Russians drew parallels between the current elite and that of Ivan the Terrible.

To some extent, corruption helped the Putin system to function, outsourcing some of the costs of government onto the population even as it fostered cohesion within the elite itself, bound to each other by complicity in illicit self-enrichment.[43] It was bad for everyone else, of course. Corruption metastasized into almost every sphere of life. Perhaps the most obvious sign of its pervasiveness was the entry into everyday speech of its distinctive lexicon. Most Russians could easily have told you the difference between *raspil*, *otkat* and *zanos*: *raspil*, 'sawing off', refers to money made through fraudulent state contracts; *otkat* is a kickback; *zanos* is a regularized cash tribute, either a flat fee or a proportion of turnover.[44] In December 2010, anti-corruption campaigner Aleksei Navalnyi even launched a website called RosPil, where users could scrutinize state contracts for the inevitable rake-offs. That same month, word leaked out about a 74-hectare estate by the Black Sea reportedly built for Putin himself, complete with pseudo-neoclassical palace, amphitheatre, sports complex and three helipads. The news was scandalous but unsurprising: aerial shots of the enormous mansions belonging to government officials and well-connected *biznesmeny* had long been a staple of blogs and Twitter feeds.

The Russian elite were not keeping their wealth all for themselves, though: they shared some of their good fortune with their relatives. Over the years, investigative journalists in Russia have repeatedly mapped out a web of nepotistic connections spanning the worlds of money and power. In 2007, for instance, *Kommersant-Vlast'* magazine listed three dozen examples of family relationships in government structures and state-owned enterprises – fathers and children, siblings, husbands and wives, in-laws, uncles and nephews. Ten years later, *Meduza* carried out a similar investigation. The first of these reports found that the two sons of Nikolai Patrushev, head of the FSB from 1999 to 2008, were respectively vice-president of the majority state-owned Vneshtorgbank and an adviser to the board of the state oil company Rosneft. By 2017, one had moved to Rossel'khozbank while the other was ensconced at Gazprom. Igor Sechin's daughter Inga was married first to the son of Vladimir Ustinov, prosecutor general and then minister of justice, and later to a former vice president of VTB bank.

Dozens more such family connections between government and the business world could be added to these. The daughter and son-in-law of Aleksandr Khloponin, the former Norilsk Nickel chairman who was federal envoy to the North Caucasus from 2010 to 2014, led companies dedicated to promoting business in that region; the son of FSB director Aleksandr Bortnikov was a senior vice president at VTB bank; Sergei Ivanov, son of the Putin ally of the same name, was president of the diamond company Alrosa; and so on.[45] The phenomenon extended from the national down to the local level: often, the children and spouses of regional leaders would be placed in charge of the leading firms in the area, in some cases turning both political power and economic activity into a single family concern.

Though nepotism was far from unknown under Soviet rule, its scale never came close to that reached in the Putin era, when familial ties became a mechanism for inheriting social rank, much as they had been in tsarist times. The steady stream of revelations about the riches of government figures and their families fuelled a quietly mounting popular anger, directed above all at the ruling United Russia party. At first this took the form of dark humour. In April 2011, the newspaper *Vedomosti* ran a story about the wealth and power accumulated by the children of United Russia officials under the sarcastic headline 'They Were Just Very Lucky'. Around the same time, Navalnyi famously described United Russia as 'the Party of Crooks and Thieves', prompting some creative reinterpretations of the party's logo. In one, the iconic Russian bear was making off with a bagful of cash; in another, the beast had its hand in a giant honeypot. But soon the party's well-known corruption prompted more active opposition, and became a central focus for the protests that erupted in December 2011 – as much as, or in some cases more than, Putin himself.

Corruption continued to be a prominent theme after Putin returned to power in 2012, and was the subject of a string of investigations made public by Navalnyi's Anti-Corruption Foundation (FBK) – in retaliation for which Navalnyi himself was prosecuted several times. In March 2017 and again in June, corruption was once more the spur for rallies in dozens of Russian cities; although the main target this time was the riches accumulated by Dmitri Medvedev, many of the protesters aimed their rhetorical fire at Putin. In this, the protesters were far from alone: according to a March 2017 survey by the Levada Centre, a quarter of those polled thought Putin was 'fully responsible for the scale of corruption', and two-fifths found him responsible for it 'to a significant degree'.[46]

There can be little doubt that a small number of people profited immensely from their access to power, and that a coterie of individuals around Putin did especially well. As the Russian analyst Dmitri Trenin pointed out in 2007, 'It would not be much of an exaggeration to say that Russia is run and largely owned by the same people.'[47] In addition to figures such as the Rotenberg brothers and Gennady Timchenko, there were the members of the 'Ozero' dacha co-operative, founded in 1996 by Putin and seven others, including Yuri Kovalchuk and Nikolai Shamalov, who were also on the US and EU sanctions lists. In 2016, the cellist Sergei Roldugin, a close friend of Putin's, was revealed to be nominally in charge of $100 million worth of assets, according to information leaked in the 'Panama Papers'; denying allegations that he was safeguarding the money for Putin, Roldugin breezily affirmed that he was 'rich with the talent of Russia'.[48]

Yet the corruption, nepotism and 'raiding' so characteristic of the Putin era are not the malignant fruit of his rule alone, nor are they solely attributable to the vices of a few individuals. The 'kleptocracy' targeted by Western sanctions is merely the flesh-and-blood manifestation of a systemic feature: the blurring of the boundary between the state and the private sector. This in turn is the result of the particular form taken by capitalism under Russian conditions. The idea that Putin and his circle are somehow unusually crooked requires us to overlook the extent to which the entire Russian elite – from billionaire oligarchs to local kingpins – is driven by the same motives, and skilled in the use of the same predatory techniques. More importantly, it asks us to ignore the wider realities of profit-making in Russia, which are rooted in the system that was imposed in the 1990s, and which Putin consolidated after 2000. That system will not be affected by the sanctions regime, nor will it be altered in the unlikely event of Putin being removed from power before his term is up.

There is a memorable scene in Andrei Zvyagintsev's 2014 film *Leviathan*, set in a small town in the far northern Kola Peninsula, in which the town's thuggish mayor pays a night-time visit to Nikolai, whom he has ordered to be evicted from his home. Red-faced and drunk, the mayor stumbles out of his chauffeur-driven car and says to Nikolai, 'You should be able to recognize power' (*'Vlast' nado znat' v litso* – literally, 'You should know power's face'). Dmitri, the Moscow lawyer whom Nikolai has invited to help him, tells the mayor he has no right to be on private property, to which the mayor responds by shouting at Nikolai, 'You never had any rights, and never will!'

One of the leviathans referred to by the title of Zvyagintsev's film is the state apparatus, embodied in the swaying petty tyrant and his disregard for Nikolai's rights. But in the film as in Russian reality, when isolated individuals try to oppose a crooked mayor or resist a 'raid', they are also up against a far larger machinery, in which state and business, profit and power, are interwoven, each sustaining and defending the other. It is all the more formidable an adversary because it is both elusive and all-pervading, abstract and yet substantial. It is both versions of the biblical monster that haunt the screen at different moments in *Leviathan*: a black whale that surfaces forebodingly from the sea, and a bleached skeleton embedded in the sand.

CHAPTER 3

Red Bequests

WITHIN THE WELTER of commentary on Putin's Russia there is an overwhelming consensus that many, if not most, of the country's problems hinge on the persistence of the Soviet past. These holdovers can take many forms, from the physical to the psychological. They include the rusting remnants of Soviet industry – Russia has hundreds of 'monocities', towns dependent on the survival of a single factory – as well as the authoritarian instincts of the country's present-day rulers, which are widely held to be a continuation of dark precedents set by the Communist Party. More diffuse than either of these, but more insidiously powerful, is the idea that a Soviet mindset still lingers within society as a whole, a set of assumptions and habits forged by decades of submission to power that supposedly keeps Russians mired in passivity to this day.

The notion is summed up in the term *Homo sovieticus*, popularized by Soviet dissident writer Aleksandr Zinoviev in the 1980s and taken up energetically by Russian sociologists. It has since become a staple of liberal punditry in Russia and beyond. For the *Economist*, Putin's continued grip on power showed that *Homo sovieticus* was still alive, and that 'the process of dismantling the

Soviet system, which started twenty years ago, is far from over'.
Nobel winner Svetlana Alexievich announced in 2015 that 'the
"Red Empire" is gone, but the "Red Man", *Homo sovieticus*,
remains. He endures.'[1] Communism, it seems, had produced a
whole zombie subspecies whose main trait was an addiction to its
toxic past. For Masha Gessen, writing in 2017, the uncanny
survival of spectres of the Soviet era was central to the story of
'how totalitarianism reclaimed Russia' under Putin.[2]

How useful is this line of thinking for understanding the
contemporary situation? I believe the past does matter – but not
in the way most people seem to think it does. Since the 1990s, the
conventional wisdom has been that Russia's transition to capitalism has been slowed or distorted by the dead weight of the past,
and that only when the country finally shakes off the remaining
vestiges of the Soviet period will it finally be able to join the ranks
of 'normal' liberal democratic countries. These arguments need to
be turned on their head. Rather than being a hindrance, the
remnants of the Soviet past have been a massive boon for post-
Soviet Russia. We can see this most clearly if we look at Russian
society at large, which has undergone a complex set of mutations
often neglected in the general run of Western analyses, focused
single-mindedly as they are on Putin.

After the collapse of the USSR, the transition to capitalism set
in motion a process of sharp social differentiation that gave rise to
new social groups and new experiences; yet it did not instantly
demolish the previous social order, which persisted in various
forms. The coexistence of these two social structures, one under
construction within the still crumbling ruins of the other, gave rise
to a parallelism of old and new – a kind of combined and uneven
social development – which effectively smoothed the path of
capitalist transition rather than blocking it.

This parallelism of old and new social structures helps explain
some of the enigmas of post-Soviet society that have most puzzled
outsiders. Why, given the extreme deprivation most Russians were

experiencing, wasn't there more upheaval during the 1990s? Why did it take so long for opposition to Putin to emerge in the 2000s? Why did so many Russians, during the petro-fuelled boom of that decade, rush to identify as members of a rising middle class, when by most indicators they would be classed as something else?

The usual answers to these questions cite many elements – including, most obviously, the disorientation sown by the 1990s transition and the real improvement in living conditions that many Russians experienced in the 2000s. But most accounts leave out an important part of the picture: the coexistence of old and new social structures provided a stabilizing subsidy to the Yeltsin regime, which Putin then inherited. The tenuous survival of pieces of the Soviet welfare system provided a safety net, however thread-bare, that allowed millions of Russians to survive the 'transition' of the 1990s. Along with these material continuities, older social structures and categories of thinking persisted even as new ones were emerging. The overlap allowed Russians to perceive them-selves as simultaneously inhabiting both old and new social universes. This double vision softened the impact of what was in fact a sudden and traumatic process of social change. To see how this worked, we need to have a clearer idea of what kind of society emerged from the USSR's wreckage, and what it did and didn't owe to the past.

At the turn of the twenty-first century, Tatyana Tolstaya's novel *The Slynx* reimagined Russia's experience of the 1990s as a post-apocalyptic nightmare. A mysterious disaster, known only as The Blast, had wiped away all traces of the preceding civilization, returning the land to medieval conditions: tyrannical rulers, rudimentary technology, endless mud. The catastrophe had also inflicted on the populace strange mutations known as Consequences. Some had gills, others cockscombs, others still had nostrils in their knees. Consequences could be invisible or all too apparent; they could be a quirk, a handicap or a skill – some old-timers breathed fire, for instance – but they were almost never shared. Everyone, it seemed, was alone in their deformity or new capability.

This was a powerful allegory for the disorientations of everyday post-Soviet experience. People's fortunes had diverged wildly, and unfamiliar figures proliferated across the landscape, from millionaires to vagrants, petty entrepreneurs to hit men. But in one crucial sense the allegory was misleading: the social world of post-Soviet Russia was not built on a *tabula rasa*. It emerged, rather, from within the carapace of the USSR – inheriting many of the previous social order's peculiarities, and transforming them into strange new shapes.

Soviet society itself was differentiated along a number of axes. Officially, the October Revolution was supposed to have abolished class antagonism. The old possessing classes – the aristocracy, landed gentry and mercantile and industrial bourgeoisies – disappeared from the social landscape within a few short years, either killed, exiled, or merged into the wider populace in a kind of group *déclassement*. The country that emerged from the wreckage of the Civil War was still populated overwhelmingly by peasants, but the New Economic Plan in force during most of the 1920s produced a cluster of entrepreneurs and petty traders in the cities. It was only with the industrial push of the late 1920s that the ranks of industrial workers began to swell. Meanwhile, the growth of the party–state and establishment of the planned economy produced a substantial layer of *apparatchiks* and bureaucrats, not to mention secret policemen.

The new Soviet constitution of 1936, though, folded all this variety into just two categories: Article I declared the USSR to be 'a socialist state of workers and peasants'. The same year, Stalin famously characterized Soviet society as 'two friendly classes and a layer' – workers and peasants, plus the intelligentsia. The '2+1' formula would remain the USSR's official sociological

self-description for decades to come. It was based on the supposedly Marxist criterion of differences in relation to the means of
production – and since private ownership of the latter had been
abolished in the USSR, the usual class distinctions didn't apply.
But as Leon Trotsky observed caustically in late 1936, 'from the
point of view of property in the means of production, the differences between a marshal and a servant girl, the head of a trust and
a day labourer, the son of a people's commissar and a homeless
child, seem not to exist at all.'[3] The '2+1' formula, in short, threw
a broad blanket over a range of factors that set Soviet citizens apart
from one another.

Far from consisting of two homogeneous groups of 'workers'
and 'peasants', the Soviet populace was sorted into many different
compartments according to income, skills, education and gender.
Labour was rewarded to very different degrees, giving rise to
inequalities of income between unskilled manual workers and
highly trained engineers, agricultural labourers and administrators of the planned economy. Wages varied significantly by
economic sector, too, and were significantly lower in agriculture
than in industry. Then there were regional differences: wages
tended to be higher in major cities, but there were also significant
premiums to be earned from working in very remote areas such as
the Arctic or Far East (although much of that gain was eaten up by
the higher price of basic goods in such far-flung places).

Income disparities to some extent reflected different skill levels.
Yet the division between manual and nonmanual labour did not
represent the same kind of hierarchy as in Western industrialized
states. This was partly because of the symbolic importance of
industrial labour in the Soviet system, which raised the status and
pay of factory workers somewhat relative to other social groups.
But it was also because the status of nonmanual 'service personnel'
was generally inferior to that of manual workers as a whole. Though
often seen as equivalent to the West's 'white-collar' workers, the
Soviet *sluzhashchie* had far less prestige and much lower pay.

Soviet hierarchies of income and skill were also strongly gendered. The USSR had an unusually high female labour-force participation rate: 86 per cent in 1970, compared with 43 per cent for the US, 49 per cent for Japan and 38 per cent for West Germany.[4] But Soviet women, with some exceptions, tended to be clustered near the lower end of the wage and skill scale. Like women elsewhere, they were mainly employed in female-dominated sectors where wages were lower: light industry, textiles, education, health care and clerical and administrative work. At the same time, they were held at the bottom of the pay ladder in sectors where women were in the minority: metallurgy, mining, chemicals. Soviet women also had to bear the main burden of housework and child-rearing, not to mention the recurrent, time-consuming task of queuing for food and other basic consumer goods. (Their partners did not offer much assistance. After comparing the time budgets of married and single women, one scholar concluded dryly that 'the addition of a husband did absolutely nothing to ease the woman's domestic burden'.)[5]

To all of these social differences could be added further, less formalized distinctions. In response to the generalized shortages so characteristic of life in the USSR, Soviet citizens developed the range of informal practices known as *blat*, usually translated as 'pull'. These personal connections and exchanged favours meant better access to scarce food items, clothing, housing, and so on. Indeed, sometimes connections were more useful than actual money.

But perhaps the most important thing the '2+1' formula omitted was the party–state apparatus itself. Membership in the Communist Party was a mass phenomenon: the total went from 1 million in 1921 to 3.6 million in 1933, and though the Great Terror and the Second World War took a tremendous toll, by the late 1960s the CPSU had some 13 million members.[6] They were drawn from across society: some two-fifths were manual workers, and 16 per cent were collective-farm peasants.[7] Those higher up the income and status ladder were more likely to hold a Party card, but the dynamic also worked the other way around: membership tended to make for greater professional success. Belonging to the Party often conferred informal advantages too, smoothing the way in all kinds of transactions or giving access to scarce goods.

This applied especially to the core of the party–state, the *nomenklatura*, which by the 1980s comprised anywhere between 400,000 and 700,000 people.[8] For some critics of the Soviet system, the *nomenklatura* constituted a class in itself – as suggested by the title of Milovan Djilas's 1957 book *The New Class*, which painted the top layer of the Soviet bureaucracy as an elite caste floating above the rest of the population. But although it enjoyed distinct advantages relative to everyone else, the *nomenklatura* was not a closed group – it was recruited, albeit somewhat unevenly, from all sectors of society – and it did not technically own any property that it could transmit to its heirs, in the manner of an aristocracy or even a bourgeoisie. At most, the *nomenklatura* could have been called a proto-class, dedicated to preserving its collective power – which it would soon seek to convert into property.

Soviet society, then, was marked by a number of social disparities. But the basic principle behind these was not rank, as in feudal societies, or class, as in capitalist ones, but a more ambiguous, *sui generis* mixture. On the one hand, many of the socio-economic features and cultural markers that distinguish classes from one another were present; but on the other, the political hierarchy of the party–state created peculiar pressures and opportunities of its own. After 1991, this uneven social landscape did not vanish with the system that created it. Rather, it served as the basis for a new and far more drastic differentiation.

After the fall of the USSR, the dismantling of the planned economy and the Yeltsin government's free-market reforms set in motion a vast machinery for the creation of inequalities. According to World Bank data, in 1988 Russia had a Gini coefficient of 0.24, which placed it in the company of, say, Sweden; by 1993, the figure stood at 0.48, putting it on a par with Peru or the Philippines. These figures only cover officially declared income, so the actual rise in inequality was surely far greater; recent estimates based on a broader set of data show Russia's Gini coefficient doubling in five years, from 0.32 in 1991 to 0.64 in 1996.[9]

The trend was especially visible at either end of the scale: even as the oligarchs rapidly acquired their fortunes, poverty was soaring. In 1992 – the year Yeltsin initiated his 'shock therapy', including a deregulation of prices that tripled the cost of food virtually overnight – the International Labour Organization classed 85 per cent of the Russian population as poor.[10] In response, the Yeltsin government adopted a new method for measuring poverty – whereupon the figure fell to 36 per cent. (This solution is reminiscent of Brecht's advice to the GDR leadership, after the East Berlin rising of 1953, to 'dissolve the people and elect a new one'.)

What was supposed to be a temporary jolt turned into a prolonged economic slump, as Russia's GDP contracted by more than a third between 1991 and 1995 – a steeper decline than in the US during the Great Depression. According to World Bank figures from 1996, more than two-fifths of the population – some 60 million people – were living on less than $4 a day, compared with 2 million in 1989.[11] Symptoms of social breakdown multiplied: unemployment spiked, and crime and murder rates doubled in the early 1990s. Public health deteriorated with incredible speed: male life expectancy, for example, dropped by five years between 1991 and 1994.

Across Russian society, economic differences grew more prominent than ever before. The arrival of the market brought what economists euphemistically call 'wage decompression'. Soviet incomes had varied, as we have seen, depending on workers' skills, education, sector, region, gender, and degree of political privilege.

In the 1990s, the range of variation became much broader. In Soviet times, for instance, average wages in different sectors of the economy had mostly hovered within a range of 25 per cent either side of the nationwide average. Come the 1990s, wages in the 'fuel-energy complex' – oil and gas – rose to more than three times the national average, whereas trade, health care, culture and light industry saw wages tumble to between 55 and 69 per cent of the average. The sector that lost out most dramatically was agriculture, where wages collapsed to barely a third of the national average.[12]

Sectoral differences tended to translate into regional ones, given the disparities between Russia's regions in terms of natural resources and economic infrastructure. In the 1990s, the major cities and the hubs for mineral extraction fared best – Moscow above all, but also the oil cities of Western Siberia. Heavily industrial and agricultural regions, meanwhile, suffered severe declines, as did areas where the 'military-industrial complex' had dominated: the closure of one-fifth of the country's military plants between 1991 and 1993 wiped out millions of livelihoods.[13]

Another major factor driving regional differentiation was the Yeltsin government's swingeing cuts to health, education, pensions and social welfare budgets. Under instruction from the IMF, it slashed real spending by anywhere between 30 and 50 per cent. This had drastic effects on education and health care everywhere. Starved of the basic funds they needed to operate, schools began to introduce 'user fees' many parents couldn't afford; by the turn of the century, more than a fifth of sixteen- to seventeen-year-olds were not in school. Health care provision deteriorated markedly too. In the first half of the decade, as child vaccination rates tumbled and funding for much adult primary care vanished, mortality from infectious and parasitic diseases doubled, and tuberculosis cases multiplied.[14]

Cutbacks in central funding effectively dumped onto cash-strapped regional and municipal authorities responsibility for a deepening social crisis they could do little or nothing to mitigate.

Again, Moscow and resource-rich regions were exceptions. They could afford to maintain a semblance of welfare provision that was beyond the reach of depressed industrial areas or the poor, non-ethnic Russian fringes of the country – for example the republic of Tuva, on Siberia's southern edge, where by 1996 poverty rates stood at a staggering 77 per cent, more than three times the national average.[15]

These wrenching socio-economic shifts ushered in a whole range of unfamiliar social actors, developing out of new kinds of economic relationships. Property ownership played a much lesser role than the neoliberal reformers had intended, however. The privatizations of the early 1990s hadn't created a nationwide mass of shareholders, but rather an oligarchy that proceeded to pile up wealth on a scale previously unimaginable. For the bulk of the population, ownership of assets remained out of reach. Housing was one partial and substantial exception to this trend, but even here outcomes were ambiguous and uneven. Starting in 1992, the majority of the country's housing stock was divested to municipalities, who were then supposed to oversee its sale to households. In practice, about half of housing was sold in this way, mainly because legal title to an apartment brought increased costs – maintenance, services – that few were able to take on.* While a large number of city-dwellers came to own apartments they could then sell (this was an especially lucrative move in Moscow), across most of Russia there was only the most tentative kind of real estate market.[16]

Privatization of the land did not unfold as expected, either. The advocates of free-market reform had envisaged a rapid opening of the stagnant Soviet agricultural sector, breaking up state and collective farms in favour of individualized ownership, the goal being to create a layer of stolid post-Soviet yeomen. But

---

* Holding title to an apartment also exposed people to the risk of extortion; many actually sold their apartments back to the municipality after privatizing them, as a kind of juridical self-defence.

farm directors managed to obstruct Yeltsin's plans for full privatization of land – announced three weeks after the shelling of parliament in 1993 – and only agricultural supply and procurement were privatized. Many large farms remained intact, and well into the 2000s relatively few independent farmers had peeled away from them.[17]

Outside of the elite, in fact, only a tiny layer of owner-entrepreneurs emerged, amounting to no more than 2 per cent of the population during the 1990s.[18] Still, the uneven flows of cash and commerce did give rise to a myriad of traders: retailers who ran the kiosks and tiny shops that sprouted along pavements and beneath underpasses; freelance salespeople who made irregular income from deals big or small; shuttle traders (*chelnoki*), who travelled huge distances, often across international borders, to buy goods for resale.[19] The vast majority of trade was small-scale, and was often as much an expression of desperation as of entrepreneurism, a survival strategy rather than a vocation. (Moscow's sidewalks during the 1990s, for example, were scattered with pensioners selling veterans' medals, silverware and other memorabilia.) A trader who was really successful could become the owner of a small business, rather than carry on selling on someone else's behalf. But often there was no clear split between proprietors and employees: traders tended to be both at the same time.

The proliferation of commerce also created plentiful opportunities for organized crime, above all through protection and extortion rackets. Nearly all post-Soviet business in the 1990s involved side payments to obtain a *krysha*, or 'roof'. Drugs, cars, weapons and prostitution were among the many other new sources of profit. Some of the most visible beneficiaries were charismatic crime lords, but a new layer of smaller-scale crooks also thrived, drawn not only from the Soviet-era criminal fraternity, the *vory v zakone* ('thieves by law'), but also from among Afghan War veterans, unemployed athletes and former security-service personnel.[20]

Meanwhile the sudden impoverishment brought by the transition to capitalism produced a new and distinct layer of the dispossessed. The liberal reformers' assault on the Soviet welfare system cast invalids and pensioners into penury and starvation, and demobbed soldiers were turned loose into unemployment or a life on the fringes of crime. Many of the millions of ethnic Russians who 'returned' to the homeland after the fall of the USSR, lacking papers or places to live, were forced onto the streets. There are no reliable figures on homelessness during the 1990s – estimates for Moscow alone range from 15,000 to 100,000 – but rough sleeping, begging and vagrancy were more visible than ever before.[21] The 'corporations of the dying' that Walter Benjamin had seen in 1920s Moscow had returned.

The making of new social actors – oligarchs and racketeers, vagrants and shuttle traders – took place alongside what the anthropologist Caroline Humphrey has called 'the unmaking of Soviet life'.[22] The term applied in particular to three groups. Two of them had been the biggest beneficiaries of the Soviet system's egalitarian elements: the working class, and women across the social spectrum. The third was the intelligentsia, which under Communism had experienced an ambiguous combination of repressions and advancements.

The Russian working class as a whole was 'unmade' in several ways during the 1990s. The sheer weight of industry within the Soviet economy – in 1980, it had accounted for 45 per cent of employment – meant that the post-Communist crisis was bound to have a disproportionate impact.[23] In effect, what took place repeated on a far larger scale the rust belt decay seen in much of the West. Many factories shed large portions of their workforce, pushing the official unemployment rate to 10 per cent in 1996; in 2000 it stood at 11 per cent.[24] This was actually not high by post-Communist standards: Poland posted a jobless figure of

13 per cent in 1995, and the unemployment rate in Lithuania in the same year was 18 per cent.[25]

One reason Russia's figure was not higher was because miserably low unemployment benefits put many people off registering (especially since they were often not paid out anyway). But more importantly, many state enterprises responded to the recession not by shedding workers but by reducing their hours or wages; in some cases they kept people on the books without paying them at all. Under- or pseudo-employment was a crucial lifeline for millions of Russians, supplying them with at least some income and continued access to the services and welfare that large-scale enterprises still provided. This also meant, though, that millions were obliged to make up the shortfall in income by taking up a whole range of other activities: factory workers moonlighted as cab drivers, engineers sold encyclopaedias, librarians cleaned apartments.

At the same time, the collective identity of the working class was being undone. The USSR had defined itself as a 'workers' state', claiming – however rhetorically – a vanguard role in the global labour movement. The transition to capitalism, among many other things, meant a fundamental rejection of this received idea. Thanks to its association with the Communist regime, the very category 'worker' had been delegitimized at a stroke. Interviewing workers from a dozen factories over the course of the 1990s, French sociologist Karine Clément pointed to a process of what she called desubjectivation, as workers lost their sense of themselves and their place in the world. Many now refused any identification with the working class – and, often, with any social group at all; interviewees spoke again and again of their isolation, their lack of a future, their uselessness to society. 'I am unsure of everything,' said one; 'I am a useless screw in a badly built car,' said another, while others still observed that 'I am not a man' or that 'I am a person on whom nothing depends.'[26]

Even as the identity of the working class was being undermined, the foundations of the economy were shifting beneath it. The labour that had defined the Russian working class was disappearing. An exodus into the service sector had already begun, bringing with it a marked decline in the skills of the labour force: the share of skilled and highly skilled workers fell from a third to a quarter of all workers between 1994 and 2002.[27] The industrial workforce remained sizable for much of the 1990s, but the value it produced was concentrated in a handful of sectors staffed by relatively few employees: extraction of oil, gas, metals, coal.

Russian women, meanwhile, felt the full impact of that decade's 'restructuring' along several dimensions. Their historically high labour-force participation had cut both ways during the Soviet era: in many cases it brought greater emancipation, but at the same time meant an expansion of the 'double burden'. Yet a notional commitment to the idea of women as wage-earners remained in place until *perestroika*, when ideas about women returning to 'the work of motherhood', their 'purely womanly mission', began to circulate – in part as a solution to the mass unemployment that would evidently come with large-scale economic reform.[28]

Presented as a choice in the 1980s, women's ejection from the workforce became an inescapable fate only a few years later. Women accounted for a disproportionate share of the newly unemployed after 1991, as well as being over-represented among the working poor: in 1993, 70 per cent of those who had jobs and yet were classed as 'extremely poor' were women.[29] In part this was because of shrinking (and often unpaid) wages in the 'feminized' sectors of the economy. There also were many more women pensioners than men – a consequence of women's longer life expectancy and the higher toll taken among men by the Second World War – which again left women disproportionately vulnerable.

The erosion of women's role as workers coincided with their removal from politics. After the abolition of a Soviet 30 per cent quota, the number of women in key governmental and administrative roles declined rapidly. It seems almost too fitting that Women of Russia, a political party that won twenty-three seats in the 1993 parliamentary elections, disappeared in 1999, merging with a party named 'Fatherland'. This process went hand in hand with the resurgence of essentialized views of sexual difference. As Labour Minister Gennady Melikian put it in 1993: 'Why should we employ women when men are unemployed? It is better that men work and women take care of the children and do the housework.'[30] Such attitudes were nothing new, of course, either in Russia or anywhere else. But though the changes under way in Russia echoed the backlash against second-wave feminism taking place in the West, they were striking in their speed and intensity. Reversing whatever gains women had made under Communism was presented as a return to the 'natural' state of affairs.

On top of all this, Russian women were experiencing increasing levels of violence and abuse in the home. The available statistics understate the reality by some distance, but they are appalling enough: in one survey, 40 per cent of wives reported being beaten by their husbands at least once, and 27 per cent said they had been beaten repeatedly; in 1994, female homicide rates peaked at levels twenty times higher than the European average.[31] In this respect as in others, the first post-Soviet decade pushed existing trends to horrific new levels.

The intelligentsia, for its part, underwent a twofold unmaking in the 1990s. The state institutions and structures that had materially sustained it were dissolving, and the sense of collective social identity that marked it out as a specific group was dwindling. Downgrading and *déclassement* were the fate of many, especially of those from the 'mass intelligentsia' – engineers, technicians, 'specialists' – created by Soviet industrialization.

The transition to capitalism had an especially dramatic effect on the vast scientific and technical apparatus. Basic funding for research in all fields dried up, and in many cases disappeared altogether. Spending on science accounted for only 2 per cent of the government budget in 2000, and the total amount was around one-thirtieth of what it had been in 1990. Thousands of academics and technical personnel were thrown into unemployment, or continued their work on minimal or non-existent resources. Many others emigrated: according to one rough estimate, some 8,000 top-level mathematicians and physicists left the country between 1990 and 1999.[32] The experience of that decade showed that scientific and technical foundations built over generations can be eroded with dramatic speed. Having helped to turn an agrarian empire into a global superpower – complete with nuclear arsenal, space programme, advances in astrophysics and cybernetics – Russia's scientists found themselves marking time amid its ruins.

The cultural sphere is often better able to function on meagre means, and to spring back from crisis quickly. Even here, though, the impact of 'transition' was far-reaching: the withdrawal of state funding did away with thousands of jobs and an entire ecosystem of publishing. Some of the old journals and magazines staggered on, and a motley array of new ones emerged. But the advent of the market meant the disappearance of many of the networks and channels through which cultural products had been diffused.

Institutional atrophy and slumping economic fortunes helped bring on a splintering of the intelligentsia's collective sense of self. In 1993, the sociologists Lev Gudkov and Boris Dubin argued that the very idea of 'a shared intelligentsia sentiment, lending rhythm to the existence of the whole social layer', had already vanished.[33] What was taking place now was a 'powerful process of professional differentiation', as the former intelligentsia was separated out into various roles thrown up by the new market order. The 1990s boom in petty trade generated a host of low-skilled, badly paid, loosely 'cultural' jobs in advertising and sales. 'Professionalization' was also in large measure a process of deskilling and proletarianization, only partially masked by the glossy patina of the new consumerism.

At the same time, a more profound shift was under way, marking a historic break with the intelligentsia's social purpose and political orientation. Among much of the cultural and artistic elite, a long-standing identification with the people – always laced with ambiguities, to be sure – gave way to an embrace of the market forces riding roughshod over them. The bulk of the country's intellectual elite were prominent supporters first of Gorbachev's *perestroika* and then of Yeltsin. Many of the key personnel implementing the 1990s reforms – Yegor Gaidar, Chubais and others – were drawn from cultural and academic circles. In their eyes, the demolition of the Soviet system was essential to Russia's advance toward 'civilization', and they vociferously backed 'shock therapy' and the free-market reforms against any and all opposition: it was Yeltsin or the abyss.

A crucial moment came in 1993, during the president's stand-off with the Supreme Soviet. The day after the shelling of the parliament building, an open letter appeared in *Izvestiia*, signed by forty-two writers, stating that 'these dumb bastards respect only force', and urging the government to take further 'decisive measures', including the banning of Communist and nationalist parties and the closure of their newspapers.[34] Barely a year later, many of the same intellectuals took a principled stand against the bombing of civilians in Grozny; but as the former dissident Andrei Sinyavsky put it, 'The intelligentsia has not yet understood that the war in Chechnya is a direct continuation of the firing on the White House.'[35] Behind the intelligentsia's political failing, according to Sinyavsky, lay a deeper desertion of their historic popular sympathies: 'The intelligentsia, which in the past had lived with the people and shared its misfortunes to such an extent that the very term "intellectual" . . . unequivocally implied a love for the people, was today afraid of those same people.'[36]

In some cases, that fear was overpowered by contempt: in January 1999, shortly after the rouble crisis, novelist and critic Viktor Erofeev disparaged the mass of the Russian population as 'medieval creatures' who were 'dragging Russia down toward the bottom':

However one relates to it, this mass has, by the will of chance, been turned into an electorate; it has a vote, but has nothing in common with democracy. What is to be done with it? Deceive it? Wash it? Re-educate it? Wait for it to die? The last option is illusory: old people trail grandchildren, great-grandchildren behind them who will also stand on all fours . . . Only one thing remains: to put them in a concentration camp. But they are in any case already there.[37]

Such language was unusual only in its vicious directness; couched in other forms and arguments, the sentiments behind it were widespread.

How completely was the Russian intelligentsia 'unmade' in the 1990s – was it in fact slated for total disappearance? In 1994, Gudkov and Dubin concluded mournfully that the intelligentsia as currently constituted was unable to address the country's situation: 'Other groups and people, it seems, will resolve the problems that have accumulated – people who have been educated differently, with a different understanding of themselves and the world in which they live.'[38] The philosopher Mikhail Ryklin thought his entire generation had already entered the afterlife, subsisting in a zombie-like state: 'After the death of the country in which we were born, we have already become dead people, and so the death that awaits us will not be the first.'[39]

Yet neither these otherworldly metaphors nor the dislocation that had inspired them were unprecedented – as the title of Masha Gessen's 1997 book on the Russian intelligentsia, *Dead Again*, wryly attests. Epochal crises had several times threatened the intelligentsia with destruction – the Revolution, Civil War, Stalinist purges and the Second World War – before Brezhnevism all but bored it to death. Each time there had then been a rebirth or refoundation, in a novel form and changed atmosphere. Would it not emerge yet again, blinking, into the new century?

―――――

Despite all the novelties the free-market transition of the 1990s brought, the switchover from the old social structure to the new could never be instantaneous or total. The two continued to exist in parallel, with new social actors coming into being alongside the remnants of the state-socialist system. Often the latter provided a meagre guarantee of income or perhaps some basic, non-monetized services; but the little it offered was never enough, and had to be supplemented with gains from market-oriented work – potentially more sustaining, but always more risky. This meant that millions of Russians found themselves inhabiting multiple social roles. The metamorphic blurring this created was captured in Viktor Pelevin's 1993 novel *The Life of Insects*, in which people are suddenly and arbitrarily transformed – a teenager turns into a moth, a widow becomes an ant, a prostitute becomes a mosquito – and all sense of scale or causality dissolves, along with any meaningful boundary between species.

The sheer confusion the process of 'transition' generated was one obvious reason for the relative lack of protests in Russia in the 1990s. Most people were struggling to survive, and many opted for individualized solutions amid the collapse of older collectivities. Privatization also made it hard in many cases to identify who exactly should be the target of protest: in much of Russian industry, for example, the actual ownership structure was hidden behind layers of shell companies and investment vehicles. As a result, the vast majority of strikes took place in the state sector rather than the private one (education alone accounted for almost 90 per cent of them between 1992 and 1996).[40]

But there were two further factors behind the strange quiescence of the Russian population, both of them examples of the persistence of the old lending support to the new. Firstly, the way Soviet industry had been organized made a huge difference. The fundamental unit was the enterprise, and despite the many differences between them, workers and management within an enterprise had tended to present a common front – for instance, against state administrators imposing plan targets. When the planned economy began to fall apart, these basic units remained largely intact, while the fabric that held them together was torn into pieces of varying sizes and shapes. After 1991, the depth of the crisis often gave rise to a defensive solidarity between workers and management, as they strove to keep production going. In many cases this was the only way for workers to keep not only their jobs but also the housing and other basic social guarantees that were, for now, still provided at the enterprise level. Paradoxically, the end of Communism reinforced workers' dependence on the old paternalistic model.

Secondly, trade unions played an often overlooked but important role. In Soviet times, trade unions had been 'transmission belts' for the party–state, their main function being to stimulate production; they were also tasked with administering some social benefits within enterprises. In theory, the end of Communism could have made room for organizations that were more independent of management. But on the whole, the old enterprise-level unions remained in place, as component parts of the Federation of Independent Trade Unions of Russia (FNPR). Many of the personnel and reflexes of Soviet unionism were carried over – and if anything, in the crisis conditions of the 1990s the unions' dependence on management only deepened. At the national level, union leaders were soon enough made politically docile, particularly by Yeltsin's 1993 move to strip FNPR affiliates of the right to administer many social benefits.[41]

Ultimately, the trade unions were a boon to post-Soviet capital and state alike: their dwindling relevance delegitimized the idea of unions in workers' eyes, and at the same time they took up the space that a more independent, combative labour movement could have occupied. This is a very concrete example of Soviet-era institutions providing a subsidy to their capitalist successors, the maintenance of one smoothing the way for the establishment of the other.

———

After 2000, the turbulence of the previous decade – many Russians described the 1990s as *likhie*, 'feverish' – seemed to abate. Now the watchword was 'stabilization', embodied in everything from the gathering economic recovery to the 2004 creation of a Stabilization Fund in which to park the steady flow of oil and gas revenues. By this time Russia's GDP had finally regained its late Soviet level, and many of the most glaring symptoms of social breakdown had begun to fade: crime rates dropped, health indicators improved, life expectancy began to rise. It seemed to sum up the mood when an annual sociology conference, held since 1993 under the title 'Where Is Russia Going?', changed its name in 2003 to 'Where Has Russia Arrived?'

But whatever stability meant, it did not mean a fundamental reversal of the socio-economic mechanisms set in motion after 1991. Much as Putin's rule was a prolongation of the substance of Yeltsin's, so in the social realm the 2000s brought a consolidation and extension of the disparities that had appeared in the 1990s. Overall inequalities of income remained sizeable. The debt default and currency crash of 1998 didn't do much to narrow the gap: few of the super-rich kept their wealth in roubles, or indeed in Russia.* This trend continued and even accelerated under Putin: according to one calculation, by 2014 the financial wealth held by a handful of Russians abroad was equal to the total wealth of the entire population within Russia's borders.[42] As the number of billionaires continued to grow, the share of national income taken home by the bottom 10 per cent remained tiny, and actually declined after 2000, from 2.2 per cent to 1.9 per cent in 2008.[43]

In one area after another, imbalances that had emerged during the 1990s solidified in the new century. The sectoral spread of

---

* Alongside the UK and Switzerland, Cyprus was often the preferred place for wealthy Russians to keep their money, in banks as well as shell companies and trusts. This explains why the island frequently appeared in statistics as the number one source of 'foreign direct investment' in Russia.

wages was slightly less dramatic, but there was still an unmistakable ladder, with the fuel and energy sector at the top – where
workers earned around 2.7 times the 2005 national average – and
agriculture at the bottom, paid at a miserly 43 per cent of the average.[44] Pensioners did better than before: in the 1990s, many never
received their tiny monthly sums, but now the state not only paid
pensions on time, it even increased them. (This accounted for a
substantial part of Putin's support base early on.) But the gender
pay gap remained in place in the 2000s, or even grew. Across the
economy as a whole, women on average earned between two-thirds
and four-fifths of what men did, but the disparity widened the
further up the occupational hierarchy you looked: male managers
earned one and a half times as much as female ones.[45]

Regional imbalances were not reversed by the 2000s oil boom,
either: if anything, the boom exacerbated them, since oil revenues
flowed either to Moscow or stayed within the production zones.
Parts of the country were being propelled into hypermodernity,
while large swathes of it remained mired in deep deprivation.
There were huge variations within regions as well as between them.
In fact, the places that posted the healthiest-looking average wages
tended to be those with the most unequal distribution.[46] Nowhere
was this demonstrated more starkly than in Moscow, where an
expanding fleet of Mercedes and BMWs whisked the super-rich
past struggling pensioners.

The 2000s also brought a new ethnic segmentation of the workforce. Informal labour migration had been a feature of the late
Soviet period, drawing workers – mainly men, predominantly
from Central Asia or the North Caucasus – to factories, farms and
construction sites across the country. This traffic slowed after the
breakup of the USSR, when the customary routes were barred by
new national borders, but during the economic revival in the new
century, it resumed on something like the late Soviet pattern –
except that the workers were now 'foreign' and also often 'illegal',
making them much more vulnerable to exploitation. Official data

counted 1.7 million labour migrants in 2007, but this didn't include undocumented workers, who made up the lion's share of the migrant workforce; according to one estimate, labour migrants all told numbered 7 to 8 million, almost 10 per cent of the working population.[47]

The new arrivals provided a large pool of unskilled labour, toiling on construction sites, cleaning the streets, working in markets or driving taxis for abysmal wages. Xenophobia against them became widespread, from the poisonous ranting of the Movement Against Illegal Immigration (DPNI) to the casual racism of TV shows like *Nasha Rasha*, which poked fun at Tajik labourers through two characters called Ravshan and Jamshud. Known as *Gastarbeitery* – Russians adopted the German word – migrant workers formed a new layer at the base of the social pyramid.[48]

One of the most significant social developments of the 2000s was the expanded role and presence of the state. The state payroll grew from 1.1 million in 2000 to 1.7 million in 2010 – a 50 per cent increase over the course of the decade. The bulk of this growth occurred at the federal level, which accounted for about half of all government employees.[49] Their spatial distribution was crucial: outside the major cities and resource hubs, federal and local government agencies were often the main sources of employment. These functionaries were an important source of support – and of help with electoral rigging – for the regime. But the Putin system drew an even larger portion of its base from among the millions working in state-owned enterprises or in the remnants of the Soviet welfare state. Together with those directly employed in the state apparatus, they formed a category known as *biudzhetniki* – literally 'those living off the state budget', though a less ideologically hostile translation might be 'public-sector workers'. In some estimates, they amounted to almost a third of the workforce; including their families and dependents, they might even have made up a majority of the population.[50]

The intelligentsia, too, experienced its version of 'stabilization' in the 2000s. Strange as it may seem today, they were initially among Putin's most enthusiastic backers. In late 1999, when Putin was still prime minister, pollster Yuri Levada pointed out that 'no Russian leader has had such unified support among the educated, professional and artistic classes since Boris Yeltsin in the late 1980s and early 1990s'.[51] Putin's seriousness and sobriety were at this point considered assets, contrasted with the drunken fumblings of Yeltsin. The assertive, macho persona was also a core part of his appeal, especially to those lured by the idea that a 'strong hand' was needed to reel in the anarchy of the 1990s. For some, Putin even promised to fulfil the neoliberal fantasy of a 'Russian Pinochet' – the idea being that authoritarianism would somehow guarantee economic growth.*

The generalized admiration of the president became self-reinforcing, giving rise to a stiflingly conformist climate in which it became outlandish as well as pointless to criticize the authorities. This shift was rendered all the more effective by the postmodern capaciousness of the broader culture: ideas and beliefs were mashed together in wildly incongruous combinations that made their substance hard to pin down, and hence difficult to argue with or oppose. Soviet nostalgia blended with folksy echoes of medieval Muscovy; Western philosophy and critical theory were digested

---

* Their willingness to overlook the Pinochet regime's bloody record was the worst part of this fantasy – a latter-day version of the idea that fascism 'made the trains run on time'. But it also relied on a total misreading of *pinochetismo*'s economic performance. What is commonly referred to as the 'Chilean miracle' actually consisted of short bursts of growth that followed deep recessions largely caused by the regime's own policies. It took until 1989 for Chile to regain its per capita output level of 1970. In the meantime, swathes of the economy had been transferred into private hands at knock-down prices, public health care, pension and education systems had been gutted, and poverty had almost tripled. In that respect, Russia had already had its Pinochet – and his name was Yeltsin. For a substantial critical assessment of the dictatorship's economic outcomes, see Joseph Collins and John Lear, *Chile's Free-Market Miracle: A Second Look*, Oakland, CA 1995, especially pp. 243–57.

alongside Russian nationalism and religious texts. A 'sickening aesthetic atmosphere' had taken hold of the country, according to the leftist poet Kirill Medvedev, who described 'the average cultural consciousness' as 'a putrid swamp – half-Soviet, half-bourgeois – in which Pushkin, Dostoevsky, Josef Stalin, the pop star Alla Pugacheva, and Jesus Christ all lie side by side, dead and decomposing'.[52]

There was also, of course, a material basis to the cultural consensus behind Putin. The burst of economic growth in the 2000s created a glossy, flashbulb-lit world of consumption, evoked by the borrowed English word '*glamur*'. There was an ever greater need for PR experts, salespeople and advertising gurus, while the arrival of the web created new positions of its own: programmers, webmasters, bloggers. Many of these posts were poorly paid and insecure, and most 'culture workers' of the 2000s had to take on other jobs to make ends meet. But it seemed as if the predictions made in the 1990s – that the market would slot people into steadily more specialized, 'professional' niches – were being partially realized. As Kirill Medvedev put it, 'there is no intelligentsia in Russia any more. There are just fragments, moving around Moscow and the other large and smaller cities, remnants, shards'.[53]

Yet although the intelligentsia seemed to be dissolving as a distinct social category and self-conscious group, traces of its former historical function and identity lingered. A handful of cultural figures and intellectuals became increasingly uneasy with the Putin regime, and in their criticisms they laid claim, in an attenuated form, to the Russian intelligentsia's oppositional role. Anna Politkovskaia was among the courageous few who objected to the slaughter unleashed in Chechnya. Meanwhile others grew disenchanted with the tightening of Kremlin controls on the media, the rising corruption, and the hostile climate generated by various official campaigns – against 'terrorism', against NGOs working as 'foreign agents', and so on.[54]

It is striking, too, that within Russian society as a whole a series of moral-ethical assumptions about the intelligentsia persisted. In a 2008 survey carried out in the provincial city of Voronezh, more than half of respondents named 'honesty' and 'cultured behaviour' as qualities essential to a member of the intelligentsia – ahead of educational qualifications, and far ahead of professional background. Hardly any, though, questioned the intelligentsia's existence.[55] The Russian intelligentsia of the 2000s, in fact, seemed to inhabit parallel realities: in one, it had been replaced by a loose assortment of people holding 'creative', academic, technical and service-sector jobs; in the other, it retained some sense of a collective identity and purpose. Like Schrödinger's cat, it was simultaneously dead and alive. In this, its experience was representative of the broader parallelism evoked earlier: the persistence of older ideas, attitudes and expectations alongside new ones generated by the arrival of the market.

The continued presence of Soviet social structures helped to mute discontent across Russian society during the 1990s. More than an accidental, temporary overlap, the coexistence of old and new played an active role in enabling the post-Soviet order to take shape; the past gave a hidden subsidy to the present. In the 2000s, this parallelism continued to pay out for Putin. Its effects were less obvious than those of Russia's economic upturn in the new century, which brought millions relief after a decade of deprivation and crisis, and which clearly accounted for much of the regime's lasting popularity. But the Putin government also benefited from the persistence of the past, in ways that become more apparent when we look at the emergence of a 'new middle class'.

By the mid-2000s Russia was only one of a number of countries thought to be experiencing a similar 'rise of the middle class'. The BRICs, for example – Brazil, Russia, India and China – between them supposedly had a 'burgeoning bourgeoisie' some 400 million strong.[56] According to the mainstream press and an extensive political science literature, these middle classes not only drove consumer spending, they would also act as a stabilizing political force in future, blocking the extremes of left and right.* The Russian political elite clearly shared these assumptions: United Russia chairman Boris Gryzlov said in 2005 that the party would be 'relying on the middle class and acting in the interests of this class, of those who need no revolutions – either financial, economic, cultural, political or orange, brown, red, or blue'. Vladislav Surkov hailed the middle class as the country's 'silent heroes', while Putin called for measures that would expand its ranks to between 60 and 70 per cent of the population by 2020.[57]

Was there any sociological basis to these ideological fantasies? The empirical evidence was puzzling, to say the least. Between 2000 and 2008, several Russian scholars tried to gauge the size of the country's middle class using various objective criteria – income, occupational status, level of education – and also the purely subjective one of how people chose to define themselves. Measured by income alone, the middle class was thought to comprise a fifth of the population; by education alone, the figure was in the range of 22 to 29 per cent. Based on how respondents defined themselves, the figure rose to between 40 and 80 per cent. But when all the different measures were used together, it dropped to between 7 and 20 per cent. Depending on the criteria used, then, Russia had a middle class consisting of somewhere between 7 and 80 per cent of the population.[58]

What was going on? Russia, of course, is far from the only place where the 'middle class', when subjectively defined, accounts for the majority of the population. In the US, for instance, the term essentially refers to what in other countries would be called the

---

* The actual historical experience of interwar Europe, when the middle classes of several countries were among the most energetic supporters of fascism, was apparently neither here nor there.

working class. In Russia, there are other factors that produce a similar effect. Firstly, consumption patterns rather than property ownership are held to be most decisively indicative of class status: spending on items like cars, white goods, clothes, imported high-end electronics, or on leisure activities like foreign holidays and restaurant meals. The emphasis on consumption means that the threshold for joining the Russian middle class is relatively low: acquiring a refrigerator or even a car is significantly more affordable than buying an apartment. State entities relying on these kinds of measurements effectively boosted the numbers; for example, the state insurance company, Rosgosstrakh, defined the middle class as those able to buy their own car.[59] It's not hard to see why the authorities would do this, given that the size of the middle class was at the time widely seen as a measure of governmental success. But, of course, it wasn't just the state that saw middle-classness as a desirable status. It was at the heart of the whole ideological climate and culture, which made the middle class the 'leading class' of the day, just as the proletariat had been in the Soviet Union.

But I believe that the parallelism of old and new also helps account for the vast size – as defined subjectively – of Russia's middle class. The country's citizens lived within multiple, overlapping social identities. Millions were able to interpret their position in the new capitalist system according to the categories of the Soviet one. Skilled manual workers, for example, had been somewhere in the middle of the Soviet status and income ladder; after 1991, manual workers steadily slipped to well below the middle of the various post-Soviet hierarchies. Yet the rise in average incomes after 2000, and the new access to consumer goods it provided, allowed many workers to claim membership in a middle class from which they would have been excluded by many other measures, most notably the criterion of property ownership.

In fact, a substantial portion of those who now described themselves as 'middle class' were working-class people of very modest means. Many of them inhabited what journalist Evgeniia

Pishchikova dubbed 'five-storey Russia', after the Khrushchev-era buildings in which much of the population still lived. Their consumption habits, she observed, involved a patient process of exploration and comparison, making each transaction significant, almost a miniature rite of passage. In a sense, this made them 'ideal consumers': 'much more loyal and informed than people who are better off than they, because for the latter, the interval between wanting to buy and making the purchase is too short'.[60] Yet at the same time, many of those who might have been defined as middle-class by their occupational status and education were suffering declining wages and even poverty. In one 2010 study, people with higher degrees accounted for a fifth of those deemed 'poor' or 'disadvantaged'.[61] These sectors of the 'middle class' were being proletarianized, even as the onetime proletariat redefined itself as 'middle class'.

There was, in effect, a mismatch between the social identities Russians claimed and their socioeconomic positions. While the majority might consider themselves members of a single 'middle class', the society that emerged in the 2000s – built on the disparities generated in the previous decade – consisted of several groups that differed hugely from one another: oligarchs, petty traders, industrial workers, migrant labourers, professionals, white-collar 'office plankton', and so on. Yet the disparities between these groups appeared less stark than they might have, thanks to the persistence of Soviet structures alongside emergent capitalist forms. This was visible to any visitor to Russia as a collision of social epochs, a kind of 'combined and uneven social development' – pensioners carrying portraits of Stalin alongside teenagers wielding iPhones; glass-and-steel skyscrapers looming over rickety barracks-style housing. It also had less tangible consequences: the lingering ghosts of Soviet social structures shielded the Putin regime from serious class conflict just as they had Yeltsin's. Much has been made of Putin's good fortune in coming to power amid an oil boom. Inheriting the 'subsidy' provided by the parallelism of old and new was yet another piece of world-historical luck.

Yet this subsidy could not last indefinitely: by definition it was temporary, the product of the continued survival of previous social structures and identities. By the 2000s what remained of Soviet institutions was becoming increasingly hollow, and the generations who had experienced life in the USSR were dwindling, succeeded by people whose lives had been shaped entirely by capitalism. This, of course, is exactly what the liberal reformers of the 1990s wished for: the final disintegration of the state-socialist system and the emergence of New Russians untainted by the mentality of *Homo sovieticus*. Sometimes this wish was expressed in decidedly ugly terms: in 1997 the liberal politician Boris Nemtsov declared that Russia must enter the twenty-first century 'only with young people'. The same year, IMF managing director Michel Camdessus told a press conference that the structural adjustment policies his organization was insisting on might well require Russia to 'sacrifice a generation'.[62] But the underlying assumption – that the past was the main obstacle on the path to a better future – has been widely shared ever since, and has remained consistent over time.

Those calling for the Soviet past to be left behind should perhaps be careful what they wish for. That past, far from being a hindrance, has actively facilitated the construction of the new capitalist order – and when the last vestiges of the Soviet world have vanished, the subsidy that first Yeltsin and then Putin enjoyed will run out. The protests that burst onto the national stage in 2011, though widely interpreted as the political coming of age of the 'new middle class', are actually better understood as signs that the parallelism is fading. The factors that helped muffle discontent in the 1990s and early 2000s are ceasing to apply; meanwhile new grievances have emerged, as well as new ways of expressing them.

There is a historical irony lurking here. Though liberal critics, in Russia and the West, insist that it is the remnants of the USSR that stand in the way of Russian progress, it may well be that much stronger opposition to the 'imitation democratic' system will emerge from the post-Communist generations, and that new forms of collective defiance will be forged not out of nostalgia for socialism but out of their shared experiences of capitalism. The future may prove more radically stubborn than the receding past.

CHAPTER 4

An Opposition Divided

I N THE WINTER OF 2011–12, tens of thousands of Russians took to the streets to protest against the rigging of parliamentary elections, and against Putin's seemingly inevitable return to the presidency. For a time, it looked as if the wave of unrest that had seized dozens of cities across the world that year – from Tunis to Cairo, Madrid to Athens, New York to Oakland – was now reaching some unlikely places. As well as large demonstrations in Moscow and St Petersburg, smaller gatherings took place across the country's vast breadth, from Kaliningrad in the west to Vladivostok in the far east, from Ekaterinburg in the Urals and Volgograd in the south to Arkhangelsk and Murmansk in the Arctic; at least 3,000 people turned out in Novosibirsk, braving temperatures of −20°C.

These protests were widely hailed as signs of the reawakening of Russia's civil society, and in particular of the country's new middle class, which had apparently 'become sufficiently affluent to assert its yearning for more accountability and less corruption.'[1] Even if the movement could do little to prevent Putin's re-election in March 2012, for many commentators the very fact of its existence meant that things could not carry on as before. The *Financial*

Times and *Economist* concluded that the protests marked 'the beginning of the end of the Putin era'.[2] But several years later, the Putin era is apparently still in full swing – and if anything, his personal dominance of the political stage has grown. His crushing victory in the 2018 presidential election secured him another six-year mandate, extending his rule to 2024.

Why has Putin been able to overcome all challenges to his authority with such apparent ease? Why, in particular, was the protest movement of 2011–12 unable to sustain itself and pose a more serious threat to his hold on power? Several factors can help explain this, the most obvious being the sharp repressive turn taken by Putin on his return to the Kremlin in 2012, as he sought to muffle the opposition, locking up many protesters in prison and landing others with ruinous fines. The case of Pussy Riot was only the best-known example: after an absurd show trial, two of the group's members were sentenced to two years in a penal colony for the briefest of punk provocations in Moscow's Church of Christ the Saviour. The Kremlin's adoption of a more aggressively nationalist stance after 2012 also played a role, especially amid the escalating confrontation with the West over Ukraine, Syria and accusations of Russian meddling in the US elections. Broad public support for its foreign policy gave the government some extra breathing room on the domestic front.

These would be significant obstacles for any opposition, let alone one operating in a political system so loaded in favour of the governing regime. Yet they don't entirely account for the difficulties the broad anti-Putin movement has had in gathering popular support. Why haven't its slogans and appeals resonated more widely across Russian society as a whole? Once again, much commentary on Russia blames this on the persistence of Soviet legacies – the unshakeable apathy of *Homo sovieticus*, who still squats in the corners of the Russian mind, putting a damper on civic action. Soviet legacies did help to stabilize the post-Soviet system, muting many forms of discontent through the 1990s and early 2000s. By the mid-2000s, though, that subsidy had begun to evaporate, as the experience of post-Soviet capitalism, rather than the memory of Communism, became the main point of reference for an increasing share of the population.

This was the context in which opposition to Putin started to emerge, and within which it needs to be understood. How and where did it develop, and what forms has it taken over time? What are its strengths and weaknesses, and what are its prospects? The answers to these questions suggest, firstly, that the 2011–12 protests were not so much the sudden coming to consciousness of a 'new middle class' as the culmination of several years' worth of tentative, smaller-scale mobilizations. Secondly, there were also crucial disparities within the anti-Putin opposition, rooted in turn in divergent explanations for Russia's ills. Thirdly, though much attention has been devoted to Aleksei Navalnyi as the figurehead of anti-Putinism, his views make him an unlikely contender for resolving the opposition's internal rifts – if anything, he may even exacerbate them. But before addressing the challenges facing the opposition, we need a better sense of where it came from in the first place.

There was remarkably little organized opposition during Putin's first presidential term, from 2000 to 2004. But after he easily won a second mandate in March 2004, garnering a mammoth 71 per cent of the vote, stirrings of dissent began to emerge. These developed along two distinct fronts: a political opposition, largely metropolitan and dominated to begin with by pro-market-reform liberal parties; and a more diffuse social opposition, arising in response to specific issues and often coalescing at a more local level. Both of these tendencies experienced ups and downs over the following decade, and on some occasions they combined powerfully. But the original gap between them persisted, and continues to pose a number of strategic problems even now.

The liberal parties' shift into opposition was in large part a result of their gradual expulsion from the official political system. This began in earnest at the end of 2003, when between them the Yabloko party and the Union of Right Forces lost forty seats in the parliamentary elections, slashing their combined representation in the Duma to seven deputies. When the next Duma elections came around in 2007, they ended up with none – partly thanks to a new 7 per cent threshold that whittled the number of parties in the Duma down to four. But the liberal parties' electoral misfortunes also reflected the tremendous discredit their embrace of the free market in the 1990s had earned them.

From this point on, liberals in Russia were for the most part peripheral to official politics, and increasingly found themselves turning to extra-parliamentary tactics. This made for some strange bedfellows: the few anti-Putin marches held in the mid-2000s were attended by a mixture of free-marketeers, human-rights advocates, and devotees of the National Bolshevik movement – a postmodern, red-brown fusion engineered by the writer Eduard Limonov that acquired a substantial youth following. This patchwork came together in 2006 in an ungainly coalition called The Other Russia, which organized a series of 'Dissenters' Marches' over the next few years. These sometimes drew decent-sized crowds, by Russian standards, but outside the major cities – principally Moscow, St Petersburg and Nizhny Novgorod – they had little resonance.

They were also largely disconnected from the scattered outbursts of discontent that were occurring elsewhere in Russian society. The most significant and, to many observers, surprising early instance of this trend came in the winter of 2004–05, when demonstrations took place in more than a dozen cities against the government's attempt to monetize a series of benefits. Pensioners played a leading role in these, leading some to dub it the 'grey' or 'chintz' revolt.[3] But the demonstrations also had very broad public support, which pushed the government to soften the reform's impact by increasing the compensation offered. Later in 2005, government moves to privatize housing and communal services – dumping the cost of capital repairs onto residents – led to the creation of local action groups in several cities, among them Moscow, St Petersburg and Yaroslavl; Izhevsk and Perm in the Urals; Tomsk, Nefteiugansk and Khanti-Mansiisk in Western Siberia.[4] Like the monetization protests, these movements did not stop the government's plans altogether but did slow their implementation. Nonetheless, the concerns of both movements were far removed from those of the liberal opposition, which criticized the Putin administration for not forging ahead more quickly with further privatizations.

At the same time – and equally overlooked by the liberal parties – a new labour movement began to emerge. Much of Russian industry remained in a despondent, demobilized state, still reeling from the rapid deindustrialization of the 1900s. But in an ironic twist, small independent unions were being set up precisely in the new factories established in Russia by Western firms. Faced with Western corporate employers, and free to act without the say-so of the FNPR bureaucracy, these unions were much more militant than their ex-Soviet counterparts: a 2007 strike at the Ford plant in Vsevolozhsk won a significant pay rise. As Simon Pirani has observed, this was a notable development because it was an 'offensive' action: workers were demanding a share of the plant's rising profits rather than struggling to defend meagre or non-existent wages, as in the 1990s. In the words of one union activist Pirani interviewed, 'people could see: companies are coming here and making a nice profit, and they are not sharing it with their employees.'[5]

Workers at plants owned by Renault, GM, Volkswagen and Heineken created independent factory committees similar to that at Vsevolozhsk. These developments did not go unnoticed by the authorities, who clamped down harshly on union activists. Valentin Urusov, who had organized 1,000 workers at a diamond mine in Yakutia, was imprisoned for four years on trumped-up drug charges, and Aleksei Etmanov, leader of the Vsevolozhsk Ford union, was twice attacked and heavily beaten.[6] The new labour movement remained small and largely isolated, and had to operate under severe pressures; but even so, its existence was a noteworthy change.

There were other displays of dissent, often around more specifically local issues. Starting in 2007, for example, cultural and civic activists in St Petersburg came together to oppose Gazprom's plans for a 400-metre-high glass-and-steel skyscraper, the Okhta Tower, to serve as its new headquarters. Mobilizing a wide range of players – architects, leading cultural figures, politicians, UNESCO – the coalition managed to block construction, forcing Gazprom to move the site for the tower several miles farther from the city.* In 2008, at the opposite end of the country, riot police had to be sent in to Vladivostok to quell protests against a government ban on the import of right-hand-drive cars.†

Still, it took a sharp economic downturn before discontent became noticeable at the national level. The first tremors from the 2008 economic crisis began to be felt almost as soon as Dmitri Medvedev took office as Putin's designated successor: oil prices dropped by two-thirds in a matter of months, going from $130 a barrel in July 2008 to $40 that December. Overall, Russia experienced the steepest drop in GDP in the G20, going from a growth rate of 8 per cent in 2007 to a contraction of 8 per cent in 2009. The recession brought a wave of factory closures, and unemployment hit 10 per cent by April 2009. By that time, almost a fifth of the population had incomes below the official subsistence level, a 25 per cent increase compared with the previous year.[7]

---

* The battles around the Gazprom building were brilliantly satirized in a Brechtian *Songspiel* titled 'The Tower' by the leftist art collective *Chto delat'*, available online.

† A large proportion of Vladivostok residents drive Japanese cars, which have the steering wheel on the right.

The downturn added new elements to the developing repertoire of protest. One was the tactic of roadblocks, a post-Soviet version of Argentina's *piqueteros*. In June 2009, the people of Pikalevo, in Leningrad region, blocked the highway between St Petersburg and Moscow to protest unpaid wages at the local cement plant, on which their livelihoods depended. They succeeded in drawing Putin's attention: in a piece of political theatre played out on TV screens across the country, the then Prime Minister publicly forced the plant's owner, metals oligarch Oleg Deripaska, to pay back wages and keep the plant open. (Putin also made a point of taking his pen back once Deripaska had used it to sign the deal.)

Pikalevo is only one of dozens of 'monocities' in Russia – towns where a single enterprise accounts for the lion's share of jobs; the largest is Togliatti, with a population of 700,000, where the government bailed out the stricken car-maker Avtovaz in March 2009. But the rescue of Pikalevo was not widely repeated, and protests in other monocities were not as successful. In Rubtsovsk in southern Siberia, for example, workers from a tractor plant held mass meetings and hunger strikes to protest the non-payment of wages and the threatened closure of the plant; the wages were paid, but the factory finally closed altogether in 2010.[8]

A second, more significant development was the emergence of movements targeting the United Russia party. In Kaliningrad in late 2009, thousands took to the streets to protest against the party's misrule, and to demand the resignation of Georgi Boos, the regional governor. As in Vladivostok a year earlier, the protests were partly driven by a government decision to impose higher import duties: cross-border trade is crucial to Kaliningrad's economy. By August 2010, the protesters had managed to force Governor Boos out – a rare political victory.

At around the same time, a different set of protesters also achieved a win, albeit a temporary one. An alliance of environmental activists and other groups, from Greenpeace Russia to anarchists and antifascists, had gathered in Khimki forest just outside Moscow to prevent the construction of a road. Some demonstrators occupied parts of the proposed route while others stormed local government offices. At one point a neofascist mob was set on the activists – and the police arrested the victims rather than the attackers. That summer, wildfires were tearing through forests across the country, wreathing Moscow itself in acrid smoke, which drew public attention to precisely the kinds of conservation issues the Khimki protesters were raising. Widespread public condemnation of the handling of the protests led Medvedev to decree that construction of the road be suspended.

The Khimki and Kaliningrad movements were signs of things to come: their ideological heterogeneity, their use of space and their focus on United Russia all featured strongly in protests a year later. The main catalysts for the 2011–12 demonstrations were popular anger at United Russia's electoral fraud, and before that at the announcement of Putin's pre-agreed job-swap with Medvedev – a 'castling' manoeuvre that displayed real contempt for the democratic process. But corruption was a crucial underlying grievance. A pervasive feature of the Putin system, it became increasingly prominent in public discourse – especially in unofficial media outlets and on the internet, where a wide and active network of LiveJournal blogs came to act as an ersatz fourth estate. The number of internet users in Russia grew phenomenally in the 2000s: from 1 per cent of the population in 1999 to 15 per cent in 2005 to 43 per cent in 2010.[9] In some ways, the web was partially compensating for the cultural infrastructure that had been lost in the 1990s. And as it would do for the Arab Spring in 2011, it provided a readymade platform for organizing media campaigns and protest rallies – its impact all the more striking given the atrophying of independent political parties and the pressure on NGOs and other civic organizations.

Long before 2011, then, scattered revolts had been taking place across Russia. They were numerically small, especially relative to the size of the country; and they were geographically dispersed, which made coordination and practical gestures of solidarity more difficult to pull off. For the moment, they remained politically disarticulated from each other. Yet there was a notable diversity of triggers and themes, from corruption to jobs, from the environment to architecture, which offered more potential points of contact with a wider public. They also had diverse outcomes: many defeats, but also some small and partial victories.

All of these experiences contributed to the breadth and energy of the 2011–12 demonstrations. The different strands of protest were able to converge at a rare moment of vulnerability for the 'imitation democratic' system. Elections remained ideologically necessary to the system's legitimation, and they had given rise to awkward transitions and crises across the post-Soviet space. This time, Russia's electoral calendar coincided with a gathering tide of discontent, and the 2011–12 parliamentary and presidential votes provided the first test of the system since the post-2008 economic downturn. Yet although this created a slender opening for Russia's multiform oppositional movements, many of the basic divisions between them not only persisted through the 2011–12 protests; if anything, they deepened.

The demonstrations of late 2011 and early 2012 drew the largest crowds since the mass marches of the *glasnost* era. The organizers of the Moscow *miting* on 4 February 2012 were clearly trying to encourage such comparisons: that had also been the date of an enormous march around the capital's Garden Ring in 1990, to protest the Communist Party's monopoly on political representation. The city authorities got the reference and refused permission for a march along the same route, insisting it be held instead in Bolotnaya Square, on an island in the Moscow River. The square thereafter became the venue for several subsequent protests, and supplied a catch-all term for the movement, too; though it was hardly an auspicious name: *boloto* is the Russian word for 'swamp'.

These protests were greeted as a 'revolt of the middle class' – an expression of discontent from those who had done well out of the petro-boom of the 2000s and were now anxious at being squeezed by recession. But the idea of the 'new middle class' was a chimera, part ideological fantasy purveyed by the state and the media, part wishful projection by the population itself. And it didn't tally with the sociological make-up of the participants in the 2012 demonstrations. As one protester revealingly put it when interviewed, 'I belong to the middle class, but it doesn't exist.'[10]

The bulk of the participants do seem to have been urban, educated and broadly liberal in their politics. A survey of a *miting* held on Moscow's Sakharov Avenue on 24 December 2011 found that three-fifths of those present held a higher degree, and almost half gave their occupation as 'specialist'. But this was by no means the prosperous bourgeoisie depicted in many Western accounts: 21 per cent said they could only afford essentials, and 40 per cent said they could not afford a car – which in effect disqualified them from the middle class, even according to one of the modest yardsticks widely used at the time.[11]

The idea that these were 'young professionals' was also belied by their generational profile: a fifth of those at the 24 December gathering were over fifty-five; a quarter were between eighteen and twenty-four. While some of those attending might well have remembered the demonstrations of 1990, many had come of age under Putin and knew nothing but the present system: the Yeltsin era would have been a chaotic blur, and the USSR something akin to Atlantis. Outside Moscow, the protests were small but heterogeneous, and some occurred in places that still lacked any of the boom-time amenities that supposedly marked a rising middle class.[12] Conversely, large swathes of those who really were members of the 'middle class' hailed by Western commentators failed to join the protests – perhaps because many of them would have been state-sector employees, the *biudzhetniki* who formed a central part of Putin's support base.

The sociological diversity of the protesters was reflected, too, in their ideological heterogeneity. 'Russia without Putin' was the hopeful banner under which many thousands marched. But beyond this basic point in common, they had very different ideas about what that Russia would look like. The protests were a medley that included not only established liberal parties such as Yabloko and Boris Nemtsov's Solidarity but also leftist groups such as the Russian Socialist Movement and the Left Front, as well as nationalist outfits such as the Movement Against Illegal Immigration (DPNI) and various groupuscules waving the tricolour of the Romanov dynasty. Alongside all these, there were also a number of social organizations: ecologists protesting the destruction of Khimki forest; the Blue Buckets, campaigning against abuses of authority by traffic police; the local franchise of the e-libertarian Pirate Party; and the avowedly 'non-political' League of Voters, which included many prominent intellectuals and cultural figures, such as the TV personality Leonid Parfyonov, ageing rock star Yuri Shevchuk and the writers Dmitrii Bykov, Liudmila Ulitskaia and Grigorii Chkhartishvili (better known as retro-whodunit writer Boris Akunin).

This bewildering political breadth was in part a product of the narrowness of the 'imitation democratic' system, which by design excluded most of the political spectrum. Yet within this diversity, the outlines of two camps emerged: a liberal one, focused on the demand 'For Honest Elections', and a smaller, leftist one, with a wider social agenda. Though the liberal camp predominated early on, its power quickly waned after it became clear there would be no re-run of the Duma vote, and that Putin would easily canter to victory in the presidential election, rigged or not. By the time protests against Putin's foreordained inauguration took place in May 2012, it was mainly the leftist groups that were still in the streets – and they bore the brunt of the repression thereafter. It was also an array of leftist groups that inspired the 'Occupy Abai' protest that took over a small park in central

Moscow in May, before being forcibly expelled by riot police after a couple of weeks.*

The differences between the liberal and left wings of the movement were apparent from early on. At the demonstration on 24 December 2011, liberal figurehead Ksenia Sobchak – a TV star and daughter of the former St Petersburg mayor who had been Putin's boss in the 1990s – told the crowd that 'the main thing is to exert influence on power, rather than to struggle for power'. She was whistled and booed by sections of the crowd, who no doubt thought precisely the opposite. When the left tried to formulate a list of social demands for the movement to put forward, the liberals rejected the idea as 'divisive'. Ultimately, 'For Honest Elections' – the liberal slogan that became the name of the umbrella organization coordinating the protests – was a demand for the system to function better, rather than for a fundamentally new system.

This disjuncture between a clear but inadequate and easily blocked political goal on the one hand, and a more expansive but largely unarticulated social agenda on the other, was a critical flaw in the anti-Putin movement, and it limited its potential reach across Russian society. But the protesters also faced tremendous obstacles which even a better organized and more widely supported movement would have been hard pressed to surmount. After Putin's return to the Kremlin, their room for manoeuvre shrank still further.

From 2012 onward, the opposition to Putin was pummelled by a combination of judicial persecution and ideological pressure. Once he had regained the presidency, Putin adopted an increasingly strident nationalistic rhetoric. A new official ideology, which placed ever greater emphasis on 'civilizational' differences between East and West, had begun to coalesce before Putin's

---

* The name derived from the statue to a nineteenth-century Kazakh poet, Abai Kunanbaev (or Qunanbaiuli in Kazakh), next to which the camp originally sprang up.

re-election as president, hovering in the background of Russia's confrontations with the US and its allies. Now it moved to the fore – and burst onto the international stage with the annexation of Crimea. But though shaped by external pressures, it was also a strategy for dealing with dissent at home, driving a wedge through Putin's opponents by framing everything in polarized, friend–enemy terms.

This much became clear even during the 2011–12 protests, which Putin wasted no time in blaming on the US State Department, describing them as another attempt at a 'Colour Revolution'. In an increasingly tense climate, those criticizing the government risked being tagged as fifth columnists. A similar logic applied to the persecution of Pussy Riot, who were portrayed not only as blasphemers against the Russian Orthodox faith with their 'Punk Prayer' but also, given the link commonly made between Orthodoxy and Russian national identity, as traitors to the motherland. Their arrest, trial and incarceration were the opening salvo in a new culture war, pitting pro-Western liberals against 'patriotic' defenders of 'traditional' Russian values – a modern-day re-run of the nineteenth-century battles between Westernizers and Slavophiles. This time it had an added dose of gender politics, since LGBT rights were presented in the Russian official media as the dividing line between Western 'decadence' and an embattled Russian 'normality'. In this atmosphere, the mere fact of being gay was reframed as an act of subversive foreign propaganda.[13]

As well as the trial of Pussy Riot, the crackdown on the protest movement brought the beating and detention of demonstrators and the arrest and judicial persecution of its leaders. On the evidence of a murky documentary, Sergei Udaltsov, head of the Left Front, was accused of plotting terrorist acts and placed under house arrest in 2013, before eventually being imprisoned the following year (he was released in August 2017). Garry Kasparov, the former chess champion and a leading liberal opposition figure since the mid-2000s, went into exile in 2013. The assassination of Boris Nemtsov yards from the Kremlin in February 2015 raised suspicions that an official investigation and trial have done little to quell. Aleksei Navalnyi was twice tried for fraud, in 2013 and again in 2014. The first trial earned him a five-year prison sentence – which was immediately suspended to allow him to run in the September 2013 mayoral election in Moscow. Up against the Kremlin-backed incumbent, Navalnyi managed to pull in more than a quarter of the vote; this was not enough to prevent his opponent from winning a first-round victory, but significantly more than had been expected.

The Moscow mayoral race confirmed an already developing tendency: Navalnyi had become the focal point of the opposition to Putin. How did he acquire this status, and what did his prominence mean for the movement as a whole? Navalnyi had become a figure of some renown in Russia long before the 2011–12 protests, thanks to his acidly ironic internet presence and his anti-corruption crusade against some of the country's most powerful companies. His best-known campaigns of that time involved buying shares in a well-connected company, and then demanding, as a minority shareholder, to see the accounts: where had the $300 million the oil company Transneft supposedly donated to charity in 2007 actually gone? Why were the oil-drilling rigs purchased by VTB Bank at a vastly inflated price simply dumped in the snowy wastelands of the Yamal Peninsula? In 2010–11, Navalnyi also set up two sites to crowdsource damning material: RosPil – from the Russian verb *pilit'*, 'to saw off' – encouraged users to scrutinize government tenders, while RosYama allowed them to report excessively large potholes.*

Since then, Navalnyi has continued to hammer away at the same theme, setting up an Anti-Corruption Foundation (FBK) in

---

* These are a historic bane of Russian life. Gogol is popularly credited with a phrase that people still regularly trot out: the country's two main problems are *duraki i dorogi* – fools and roads.

2011, which has carried out several investigations into the thievery of key members of the elite. In 2014, it published a report on the unbelievably inflated costs of the Sochi Olympics – many of the funds coming straight out of the state budget – and the following year produced a film centred on General Prosecutor Yuri Chaika and the business empire built by his sons. In March 2017, it released a documentary targeting Prime Minister Dmitri Medvedev, listing his collection of yachts and his formidable real estate holdings, which include palatial apartments, holiday homes, and vineyards in Russia and Italy.[14]

It was this report – titled 'Don't Call Him Dimon', after the diminutive nickname many Russians applied to the former president – that prompted a string of anti-corruption protests in dozens of cities in March and June 2017. The second round was larger than the first, bringing at least 50,000 people onto the streets in 150 places, according to one report. As with previous protests, many of the individual gatherings were small, but the geographical spread was impressive: several thousand turned out in cities deep in the interior – Ivanovo, Omsk, Chelyabinsk – as well as in the larger metropolitan centres. On both occasions, more than 1,500 people were arrested in total.[15] Strikingly, many of them were teenagers – too young to have participated in the 2011–12 protests themselves, but raised in the more embattled atmosphere of Putin's third term, in which the idea of contesting the system was not only regularly aired by the system's opponents, but had also come to trouble the imaginations of those in power.

Many of the strategies the Kremlin and its allies adopted to counter Navalnyi backfired. If anything, they heightened his importance, validating the tendency of Western media outlets to centre their coverage of the opposition around him. It's not hard to see why Navalnyi acquired such visibility. Charismatic, relatively young, he has a combination of no-nonsense directness and mischievous humour that has served him well in conveying his ideas, especially on social media. But his ascent quickly raised concerns within the opposition, both about Navalnyi himself and about the strategic implications of his personal prestige. In promoting this one man as its paramount leader, did the opposition risk creating its own mirror-image Putin – or worse?

Many of these anxieties stemmed from another dimension of Navalnyi's public persona: a Russian nationalism that often spilled out in chauvinistic outbursts. Having joined the liberal Yabloko party in 2000, Navalnyi was expelled from it in 2007 for helping to organize the 'Russian March', a gathering of far-right nationalists whose best-known slogan is 'Russia for the ethnic Russians!'* He was dismissive of liberal squeamishness about the connection, telling one interviewer in 2012 that 'what is discussed at the Russian March, if we abstract from the people shouting "Sieg Heil", reflects a real agenda that concerns a great many people'.[16]

That agenda notably included hostility toward migrants from Central Asia and Russian citizens from the North Caucasus. Central Asian migrant workers came to Russia in increasing numbers during the boom years after 2000; whether they came through official or unofficial channels, they remained vulnerable to extortion at the hands of the police and violence at the hands of the far right. The North Caucasus, meanwhile, had become an object of particular venom among Russian nationalists in the wake of the Chechen wars – fought, it should be recalled, to keep the region as part of the Russian Federation. All the republics of Russia's mountainous south depend heavily on federal subventions, and after the economic downturn of 2009, 'Stop Feeding the Caucasus' became a frequent slogan of far-right marches – directed not only at the lavish lifestyles of the Kremlin's placemen in the region, but also against the idea that federal revenues should go to non-Russian areas in the first place.

---

*   In Russian, the adjective *russkii* denotes Russian ethnicity, whereas *rossiiskii* is used to refer to citizens of the Russian Federation as a multiethnic whole.

Navalnyi has at different times endorsed expressions of chauvinism against both these groups, and against others too. During the 2008 war with Georgia, for example, he called for cruise missiles to be rained down on that country and referred to its nationals as 'rodents' (*gryzuny*) – a pun on the Russian demonym for Georgians (*gruziny*). He has, on more than one occasion, voiced objections to migrant workers' physical presence, complaining to one interviewer about their posture: 'They should stop sitting on their haunches! It drives me crazy.' 'I'm not against people coming here,' he added, 'but they need to behave in accordance with the generally agreed norms.'[17]

Shortly after his 2007 exit from Yabloko, he appeared in a video put out by a nationalist organization he co-founded called 'Narod' ('The People'). Breezily discussing how to deal with cockroaches and flies, he asks: what do you do if the cockroach is too big, or the fly too aggressive? At this point, an image of Shamil Basaev, the Chechen Islamist warlord, appears alongside him on the screen, and then a shadowy, bearded figure emerges from behind the camera and attacks Navalnyi with a knife; he shoots the figure with a pistol, and when the smoke clears, the message of the video appears: carrying firearms should be legalized. Of course, the video is not *actually* saying we should shoot Chechens; but it is implying they are insects. The combination of macho humour and dehumanizing rhetoric is all too familiar: it reminds you of no one so much as Vladimir Putin, with his vow to 'wipe out the terrorists in the outhouse'.

These ugly sentiments rightly caused a great deal of unease, even among some of Navalnyi's supporters in Russia and his boosters in the West – prompting Navalnyi himself to murmur belated apologies for some of them. Critics of Navalnyi, meanwhile, seized on such statements to denounce him from a range of ideological perspectives: Russian officialdom labelled him a fascist demagogue, some liberals condemned him as yet another charismatic leader figure in a sombre tradition, while some on the left identified him as 'Russia's Trump'.[18]

Navalnyi's mixture of chauvinism and entrepreneurial frustration with the way Russia is governed makes him a peculiar synthesis of post-Soviet trends: an Orthodox Christian, he professes his love for the fatherland while admiring the corporate governance of Western blue chip companies. In the run-up to the 2018 election, many argued that Navalnyi's status as the opposition's *de facto* leader was so incontestable that any alternative to Putin had to be built around him, whether one liked it or not.[19] But in December 2017, having been convicted of fraud for a third time a few months earlier, Navalnyi was barred by the courts from taking part in the following year's presidential contest. How well he would have done is open to debate – would he have improved on his 25 per cent–plus in the Moscow mayoral race, or performed in line with the polls, which by late 2017 were putting his rating in the miserable single digits? But either way, he has remained an established feature of the political landscape, and a gathering point for various kinds of discontents.

For the Russian left in particular, Navalnyi has presented an especially acute dilemma. On the one hand, the left could refuse to join forces with the pro-Navalnyi sections of the opposition in protest at his chauvinism. But this would mean forfeiting any chance of influencing the movement in future, and of harnessing its real popular energies for progressive ends. On the other hand, it could ally itself with Navalnyi – with whatever caveats and critical distance. But this would bring the risk of being tainted by association with his reactionary views. The question is at once a tactical and a strategic one – both a matter of manoeuvring to shape the political agenda in the short run, and of framing clearly what kind of country they want to create in the longer run. Given the sheer numerical weakness of the Russian left, it might make sense to forge provisional, temporary alliances in the service of certain goals – in this case, assembling a serious political challenge to Putin. In the meantime, the left could still go about the slow, patient work of building a broader social base for a genuinely progressive movement. This, indeed, seems to be the approach many activists in Russia have taken, including those on the left and in the range of social movements evoked earlier. Given the scale of the tasks confronting these groups, and the very real threats of physical violence and incarceration they face, they could be forgiven for seeing flexibility as a precondition not so much for success as for survival.

Yet the distinction between short-run tactical compromises and long-run perspectives may not be so clear-cut. What one does in the now is interlinked with what kind of future one imagines, current commitments and ideals mutually inflecting and reshaping each other. For the Russian opposition, the problem has been that certain key commitments are already implied by the very fact of Navalnyi's prominence. The anti-Putin movement hasn't worked out a programme through a process of negotiation; rather, it has often had to respond to an agenda defined to a large degree by and through Navalnyi. This in turn raises another critical problem: what kind of alternative would Navalnyi represent for Russia?

Throughout his career as a public figure – from LiveJournal entries in the 2000s to his spearheading of the 2017 protests – the core of Navalnyi's popular appeal has been his relentless opposition to corruption. But this does not in itself amount to a political philosophy, let alone a programme. For that, we need to look beyond Navalnyi's activism. We can get a good idea of the policies he might put forward from the platform agreed by his Party of Progress in 2014.[20] Some of its recommendations are aimed at undoing the most autocratic features of Putinism: reductions in the power of the presidency; shortening of presidential terms back to four years; introduction of stricter term limits; lowering of the threshold for parliamentary representation, and easing of restrictions on registering parties.

Elsewhere the document calls for basic political and civil rights – freedom of the press, freedom of assembly, religion and expression – that have been curtailed under Putin. Legal reforms would seek to protect the independence of the judiciary, and to make the police more accountable to the citizenry. Authority should be decentralized, devolving more power to the regional and municipal levels. The current 'bias' in federal funding for the North Caucasus should be brought to an end, though the means for doing this remain unspecified. On migration, the document calls for a visa regime and quotas to be introduced, first and foremost for the Central Asian republics, in order to moderate the currently 'uncontrolled' flow of migrants.

In the realm of foreign policy, the document calls for a rapprochement with the West, which it sees as sharing basic strategic interests with Russia: a reduction in global tensions, the struggle with terrorism, freedom of trade. Behind these overlapping interests lies a deeper commonality of values: the text describes Russia as 'part of European civilization, where ever greater significance is given to the freedom, self-respect and responsibility of the individual, and the interference of the state in various spheres of human interaction is less and less necessary'. This is, of course, a highly tendentious reading of what would constitute 'European' civilization, if such a thing existed: it refers at most to the dominant ideological tendency of the past thirty years, derived from the ideas of Friedrich Hayek and Milton Friedman and put into practice by Thatcher, Reagan and their many heirs.

Indeed, the Party of Progress platform firmly places it in this neoliberal lineage in the social and economic spheres, with prescriptions drawn from the standard repertoire of the US and European centre-right. Russia's ills are held to stem from the overweening power and reach of the state, and should be remedied by deregulation, cutbacks in the number of government functionaries, and privatizations to reduce the weight of the state in the economy. The current flat income tax rate should be supplemented with wealth and property taxes, but there should be no shift to progressive taxation, since this would penalize the middle class. Welfare should be targeted and recipients rigorously means-tested, and whatever social guarantees the state provides should not interfere with economic growth and competitiveness. Pensions should be switched to a defined-contribution basis rather than the current defined-benefit system, and the pension age gradually raised. Private–public partnerships should be encouraged in health care, education and infrastructure.

This is, of course, a familiar set of recipes. In some ways, the Party of Progress platform is a digest of the last three decades of conventional Western social and economic policy. The only real surprise here is seeing these ideas being actively recommended almost a decade after they led the world into a pervasive crisis from which no exit is in sight. If put into practice in Russia, they would likely worsen the situation for millions. As the experience of the West has shown, means-tested benefits and 'targeted' welfare have functioned as a way of withdrawing social guarantees, pulling the rug out from under a whole swathe of society while subjecting them to onerous and humiliating bureaucratic burdens. Public–private partnerships would saddle the public with colossal debt while pouring revenues into the pockets of private companies. More privatizations would amplify the already tremendous imbalances in wealth and power. And raising the pension age in Russia without first drastically improving health indicators would stretch most people's working lives beyond their life expectancy.

But the problem is not simply that these ideas have been found wanting elsewhere. More importantly, many of them either extend or intensify free-market prescriptions that have already been tried in Russia as well, and have sparked multiple protest movements both before and after the 2011–12 cycle. Since Putin's return to office, in fact, the small-scale mobilizations evoked earlier have continued. Starting in 2013 there were protests against reforms imposing austerity – officials called it 'optimization' – in the healthcare system, followed in 2014 by protests against cuts to education funding. More surprising were the nationwide actions that began in November 2015 as long-distance truck drivers, *dal'noboishchiki*, protested against increased freight taxes. These were to be levied through a new electronic payment system called Platon, which happened to be owned by the son of Putin's friend Arkady Rotenberg – a connection which for many encapsulated the injustice and crookedness of the whole scheme. The system was introduced all the same, but the truckers renewed their protests in 2017 – having formed a new trade union in the meantime. The independent labour movement remains active, though it has come under severe judicial pressure: since 2017 both the truckers' union and the Inter-Regional Trade Union 'Workers Association' (MPRA), led by former Ford unionist Etmanov, have had to battle against an official designation as 'foreign agents'. Environmental actions, too, continue: in 2017, a group of 'guerrilla pensioners' in Karelia managed to block a mining company's bid to fell a forest.[21]

The gap between the policies proposed in the Navalnyi-inspired platform and these wider social realities is only the latest variation on the split that has run through the anti-Putin movement from the outset, and remains unremedied: the disconnection between its political and social components – the one focused on the removal of Putin, the other on the malign consequences of the system over which he presides.

There are many reasons for the persistence of this disparity between the different components of the opposition. But the basic fault line was created by different understandings of the source of contemporary Russia's ills. For Navalnyi and many others aligned with him, the post-Soviet economy has not thrived as it should because, as Navalnyi himself has put it, 'The source of money is not entrepreneurial talent . . . [rather] money is born from power.' Genuine entrepreneurship is stifled because 'Komsomol bastards' have been able to profit from political clout or personal networks.[22] From this perspective the fundamental problem, of which the

Putin system is only a symptom, is that Russia's transition to capitalism is incomplete; a cleaner, fairer, more transparent market-based order would eliminate the distorting statist legacies that have held it back. The Party of Progress, in its attempts to loosen the Russian state's hold on the economy, in many respects aims to continue and complete the work of the free-market reforms of the 1990s.

Yet this line of thinking rests on at least two mistaken assumptions. One is a belief in an abstract, idealized capitalism that could incarnate free-market principles in an undistorted fashion. No such model exists: there is no capitalism, no market, no economic activity even, outside of history. The 'capitalism' Russian oppositionists aspire to emulate is the product of the specific and diverse histories of Europe and the US, shaped by concrete events and flesh-and-blood people. A related but still more consequential error is the idea that what Russia has now is not – or is not yet – capitalism, and that the failure to establish 'proper' capitalism is what accounts for the perversions of the present. But many of the characteristic features of the Putin system are directly descended from the post-Communist order installed in the 1990s, which Putin has consolidated and prolonged. The foundational purpose of this 'imitation democratic' system was the establishment of capitalism, and it owes its subsequent shape to the desire of Russia's rulers to maintain that initial commitment and defend their gains. Capitalism, in short, has predominated in Russia for the past three decades, and what many Russian oppositionists see as symptoms of its absence are, instead, structural features of the kind of capitalism the country has.

An opposition that remains committed to fundamental misunderstandings of this kind risks misdirecting its efforts. In seeing the Putin regime as the sole source of the country's political, economic and social afflictions, it mistakes symptoms for causes. Unless and until it acknowledges that the ultimate source of these afflictions is the form Russian capitalism itself has taken, even if it

changes the faces in the Kremlin it will not change the mechanisms that do the most severe and long-lasting damage to the
country. The concerns that observers in Russia and elsewhere have
raised about Navalnyi being a dangerous chauvinist are valid
enough on their own. But even if he were not, his stated policies
would leave so much of the substantive content of the post-Soviet
system in place that, for the majority of Russians, it would be hard
to say what had changed.

It's that basic disconnection between the political goals of the
Navalnyi-led opposition and the social concerns of the broader
array of movements that remains, in my view, the great weakness of
the anti-Putin opposition as a whole – and it's only by bridging
that gap that the movement will be able to present a viable challenge to the system in the longer run. For that to take place, Putin's
opponents need to do more than imagine another way for Russia
to be governed and for its entrepreneurs to make money: they
must address the questions of what kind of lives and livelihoods
Russia's citizens are entitled to, whose needs are to be prioritized
and what, in the end, the purposes of economic growth are. They
would need, in short, to envision an alternative model for Russian
society. This would be an extremely tall order for any opposition
movement – and not just in Russia. But there as anywhere else, it's
only by keeping one eye on that horizon that progress toward
genuine change can be made. For now, that remains a distant
prospect, and whatever small gains a progressive anti-Putin movement might make at home are likely to be overshadowed by events
on an increasingly tense and turbulent international stage.

CHAPTER 5

After the Maidan

THE EVENTS OF THE PAST few years have created a glaring divide between Russia and the West. How and why did this happen? In the West, the story of how relations with Russia descended to their current abysmal level is often told as one of an ominous drift, under Putin, back toward a Soviet-style showdown between Moscow and its former adversaries – prompting many to conclude that the two sides found themselves waging a 'New Cold War'. From this perspective, the clashes of the 2000s, especially the Russo-Georgian war of 2008, were early warning signs of Russia's steady regression to Communist-era thinking, after the liberal interlude of the 1990s. Everything that has happened since 2014 – the annexation of Crimea, sanctions, clashes over Syria, allegations of Russian meddling in the US presidential election – has merely conformed to a sinister pattern that was already in place.

But there are several things wrong with this story. One is the substantive continuities between Putin's rule and that of Yeltsin; indeed, both regimes should be seen as successive phases in the life cycle of a single post-Soviet system. Secondly, the idea that Russia has wilfully reverted to hostile Soviet type on the international stage rests on an extraordinarily one-sided view of what has actually happened since 1991 – one that ignores the West's own actions, which have forcefully shaped Russia's decisions. Indeed, the fundamental fact that has defined relations between Russia and the West since the end of the Cold War is the huge imbalance in power and resources between the two sides. All other geopolitical calculations have flowed from it – including both the West's impulse to drive home its advantage through the expansion of NATO, and Russia's growing resentment of that process, as well as its inability to halt or reverse it.

Those who point this out are often depicted as Kremlin stooges, as if to note a disparity in power between the two parties were somehow to take the weaker side. To be sure, Putin has found sympathizers in unlikely places – on the left as well as the right. Some, for example, insisted on seeing Russia's bombing of civilians in Syria as part of a 'counter-hegemonic' design. But there is a huge distance, politically and ethically, between measuring how much power Russia really has and defending what Putin does with it. One of the effects of the escalating rhetoric of the 'New Cold War' has been to conflate the two, and thus to prevent any serious discussion of the actual international balance of power. Yet it's impossible to understand the course of relations between Russia and the West over the past three decades without taking the disparity between the two sides into account.

Once we do, a rather different picture emerges. The events of 2014 and after are indeed highly significant in global terms, not because they confirm any atavistic tendencies on Russia's part but because they represent a break with the dominant foreign-policy framework of the post-Cold War period. They signal the demise of the idea of Russian integration or alliance with the West. For much of Russia's modern history, it was relations with Europe and, later, the West more broadly, that shaped the way the country's leaders imagined its role in the world – whether that meant being engaged in inter-imperial competition, locked in Cold War antagonism, or set on post-Soviet dreams of convergence.[1] After 1991, the Russian elite tended to see the country's future as lying either alongside or within the liberal internationalist bloc led by the United States. This commitment first gained ascendancy in the Kremlin under Gorbachev, and reached its peak during the Yeltsin years; but it remained substantially in place under Putin and Medvedev too – lasting much longer than is assumed by the general run of Western media commentary. It was only finally undone in the wake of the Ukraine crisis, to be succeeded by a more combative vision.

The downfall of the pro-Western idea in Russia represents a major geopolitical watershed in its own right. It marks our entry into a period of great uncertainty, in which relationships between the major world powers are likely to be less stable and less predictable than they have been for a lifetime. The consequences of this will resonate far beyond the scandals over Russian influence buying and electoral meddling that have occupied so much attention in the US and Europe over the past few years. Indeed, they will strongly affect how the rest of the twenty-first century unfolds. All the more reason, then, to get a clearer understanding of how and why relations between Russia and the West deteriorated as they did.

The end of the Cold War brought a sudden and dramatic downsizing for Russia, in several respects. The most literal one was territorial: when the red flag was lowered from above the Kremlin at the end of 1991 and replaced with the tricolour of the tsars, the Russian president ruled within borders that roughly matched those of 1700. The fourteen other republics that had composed the Soviet Union became foreign countries overnight, and though Russians until recently referred to the ex-USSR as the 'near abroad', these states have moved inexorably out of Moscow's orbit in the years since the Soviet Union's fall – a historic reversal of centuries of regional dominance. Outside Russia the break-up of the USSR was often depicted as the resumption of a long process of decolonization, but in Russia itself, the national sovereignty of former Soviet territories often produced a confused post-imperial resentment.

The sense of a reduction in Russia's stature was also fuelled, of course, by its rapid pullback on the global stage. By the mid-1990s Moscow had withdrawn its troops from Eastern Europe, the Transcaucasus and Mongolia and had all but shut down its bases in Cuba and Vietnam. Over the course of that decade Russia underwent what a former Soviet military analyst described as 'one of the most stunning demilitarization processes in history', shedding two-thirds of its armed personnel and slashing defence spending by 95 per cent.[2] The USSR's military-industrial complex had notoriously swallowed an estimated 15 to 20 per cent of Soviet GDP; for most of the 1990s, the equivalent figure for Russia was about 4 per cent of a far smaller GDP. But perhaps the true measure of Russia's military slump came in the First Chechen War, when a poorly equipped, ill-trained army of conscripts – many of them teenagers – was sent to crush separatist militias and was instead fought to a stalemate in the ruins of Grozny. One of the most acute contemporary assessments of that war dubbed it the 'tombstone of Russian power'.[3]

Compounding these reductions in geopolitical influence and military weight, the 1990s also saw Russia slide down the global economic hierarchy – a shift made all the more pronounced by the simultaneous rise of China and East Asia, which rapidly overtook Russia as economic powers. At the start of the decade, the GDP of the Russian component of the USSR had been one and a half times that of China and almost double that of South Korea, but by 2000 stood at only 20 per cent and 46 per cent of each respectively. The figures relative to major economies over the same period were even worse: a drop from less than 10 per cent of US GDP to a mere 3 per cent, and from 17 per cent of Japan's to 5 per cent. At the dawn of the new century, in absolute GDP terms Russia ranked lower than Brazil or India and only slightly higher than Turkey.[4]

Post-Soviet Russia, then, though it was spared the total disintegration that other fallen empires have suffered – Austria-Hungary, for example – nonetheless lost much of what had made it a force of global stature. Moscow could no longer project power much beyond its borders. Its ideological reach was similarly circumscribed. Meanwhile, its economic position was disastrous and worsening relative to most of the world's. Yet at the same time, it retained many of the attributes of a state much more powerful than it now was. It still had a UN Security Council seat and a vast nuclear arsenal. It had a large, if increasingly dilapidated, military-industrial complex, and the remains of a significant scientific-technical apparatus. Less tangible but also important were cultural factors: a language used extensively outside its new borders – including by a 20 million-strong ethnic Russian population that was now effectively a diaspora – and a literary and artistic patrimony of global renown.

The disparity between limited resources and lingering pretensions was the source of much confusion and frustration, the foundation for a great-power nostalgia that was often divorced from any real attachment to the Soviet system itself. Subjectively, many Russians – including a good portion of the policymaking elite – retained a superpower worldview, feeling the areas where the country's strength had diminished as so many geopolitical phantom limbs. They had not yet become accustomed to the world they now inhabited, nor had they adjusted their thinking to the demands of an international system that was being forcefully reshaped by their former adversaries. From the very start of the post-Soviet era, a significant gap opened up between Russian assumptions and Western ambitions.

The diminution of Russia's significance on the world stage coincided – not by chance – with the period of maximum alignment between the Kremlin and the West. An affinity with the West had begun to take root among the Russian intelligentsia and scattered members of the party–state apparatus as early as the 1960s. But it was only with Gorbachev's rise to power that the 'New Thinking', as it was known, was installed as the guiding principle of Soviet foreign policy.[5] Gorbachev went much further than *détente*, speaking in 1989 of building a 'common European home'. He envisaged an ultimate integration of Russia and the Warsaw Pact countries into a harmonious bloc of broadly social-democratic states, a kind of Greater Scandinavia. Under Yeltsin, however, what had been an impulse toward convergence turned into a project to make Russia into a 'normal' liberal democracy, firmly under the tutelage of the US. If Gorbachev and his Politburo had stunned their Cold War interlocutors with the concessions they had been willing to make, Yeltsin's government went still further, at times seeming to abdicate altogether from having policy goals of its own. In 1992, when asked by a visiting Richard Nixon what his country's particular interests now were, Russian foreign minister Andrei Kozyrev could not identify any, and even asked Nixon to help him out with some suggestions.[6]

The lurch toward the West was not only a matter of admiration for capitalism; it was rooted in a deeper set of prejudices and teleologies. Kozyrev spoke of Russia's desire to join what he called the 'community of civilized states' – with the implication that the West itself was what constituted 'civilization' and that the non-West was backward, even barbaric.[7] This attitude was soon reflected in Russia's policy stance, as Soviet-era ties to China, India and the Arab World were largely neglected. Still more crucially, Russian policymakers began to include in the non-West most of the former USSR – viewing those countries as burdens they fortunately no longer had to carry. In the summer of 1993, Russia unilaterally scuttled the rouble zone that had been agreed during the breakup of the USSR, sending the successor states scrambling to print new currencies even as Russia's price deregulation made rouble inflation spiral. Moscow also raised new tariff barriers, which frayed still further what had already been a meagre lifeline for the other ex-Soviet territories. In the 1980s, Russia had accounted for around half or more of every other republic's trade – almost three-quarters in the case of Ukraine.[8] The planned economy that had disintegrated in 1991 had been an interdependent whole, but now most of the USSR's components were left with senseless fragments, which helped make the 1990s' economic slump far deeper in these countries than in Russia.[9]

The Kremlin's early turn away from the rest of the former USSR also accelerated a centrifugal dynamic among the ex-Soviet states themselves. For several of the republics, sovereignty had come as a surprise – the Central Asian states barely managing to squeeze in declarations of independence before the USSR fell apart. All the Soviet Union's former components, apart from the Baltics, soon joined the 'Commonwealth of Independent States' created by Russia, Ukraine and Belarus in the 1991 Belovezha agreement that dissolved the Soviet Union. But although the CIS was, in Russian, actually called a *soiuz* – a 'union' as the USSR had been – it was from the outset intended to be a far looser form of association. Indeed, it was widely described even at the time as a mechanism for 'civilized divorce', in the words of Ukrainian president Leonid Kravchuk – a way to preserve appearances, perhaps, while living separate lives.[10]

Beneath the CIS's forms, symbols and occasional pacts, what took place over the next few years was a process of regional disintegration, as each of the former Soviet states consolidated itself as a separate sovereign unit, the policy interests and trade links of each pulling in a different direction from the others. This development was all the more striking given the many basic commonalities between them, especially in the political realm. Across most of the post-Soviet space, 'imitation democratic' regimes similar to that of Yeltsin came to power – from Lukashenko's in Belarus to Nazarbaev's in Kazakhstan – and developed along comparable lines, each experiencing its own version of the conflict between president and parliament that Yeltsin resolved with tanks in 1993.[11] Yet despite these parallels, the very fact of sovereignty seemed to create widening divergences between the ex-USSR's parts.

The centrifugal momentum continued even after Kozyrev's removal in 1996 brought a change of direction in Russian foreign policy. The disasters of 'shock therapy' had undermined Yeltsin's popularity and boosted the electoral fortunes of the Communists and nationalists in the 1993 and 1995 Duma elections. They also drained what little support there had been for the Westernizing line. Kozyrev's replacement, Evgeny Primakov, a Middle East specialist and former spy chief, represented a rather different school of thought – a statist tendency that aimed not to join the West but to balance against its overweening power. The recalibration of policy meant cultivating ties with East and South Asia and the Middle East, and reconnecting with Russia's former Soviet neighbours in the hopes of forming a regional support base.[12] Yet this still did not represent a fundamentally anti-Western orientation: even if the goal was to revise the terms on which Russia engaged with the West, that engagement remained the central focus of policy.

Primakov's new course certainly proved more popular than Kozyrev's, and he continued it during his brief stint as prime minister in 1998–99. But its success was premised on the West's willingness to treat Russia as an equal on the world stage, as something like the great power it no longer was. This was a delusion the US and its allies were not prepared to share. The fundamental fact of the post-Cold War order, after all, was the colossal imbalance between the US and all other powers. With less than 5 per cent of the world's population, by the mid-1990s the US accounted for a quarter of its total economic output, a fifth of its manufacturing, and two fifths of its military spending – in dollar terms committing more to its armed forces than the next eleven highest-spending countries combined.[13] Flushed with Cold War victory and now holding uncontested sway over the globe, the lone superpower had a free hand to remake the international order as it saw fit. A crucial component of the strategic design that took shape in the first half of the 1990s was a bid to nail down Washington's new advantage by extending NATO eastward, to the former Soviet satellites of

Eastern Europe. This project shaped the foreign-policy environment in which Russia has had to operate ever since, so it is worth delving further into its origins and the motivations behind it.

The idea of expanding NATO was already in the air even before the Soviet Union fell apart – despite assurances given to Gorbachev by several Western leaders that 'nothing of the sort will happen'.* The organization's London summit of July 1990, for example, issued an invitation to the Warsaw Pact countries to begin diplomatic exchanges. But the policy only gathered real momentum under the Clinton administration, coalescing as a priority by 1993–94.[14] Its main proponents within the administration saw it as very much part of a politico-economic project to reshape Eastern Europe along liberal capitalist lines.[15] In September 1993, Clinton's national security adviser, Anthony Lake, announced that 'we have arrived at neither the end of history nor a clash of civilizations, but a moment of immense democratic and entrepreneurial opportunity . . . The successor to a doctrine of containment must be a strategy of enlargement – enlargement of the world's free community of market democracies.'[16] In this neo-Wilsonian vision of an expanding free-market Pax Americana, the prospect of NATO membership was a means of pressuring East European governments to keep up the pace of 'reform'; indeed, first among the 'Perry Principles' laid down for would-be NATO members at the time by US defense secretary William Perry was a commitment to 'democracy and markets', with 'defence of other allies' much further down the list.[17]

---

* The words of British Prime Minister John Major. According to declassified documents published in 2017, similar assurances were given to Gorbachev by US Secretary of State James Baker – using the now famous formula 'not one inch eastward' – as well as by German Chancellor Helmut Kohl and his Foreign Minister Hans-Dietrich Genscher, French President François Mitterrand, and NATO Secretary-General Manfred Woerner. See Svetlana Savranskaya and Tom Blanton, 'NATO Expansion: What Gorbachev Heard', *National Security Archive Briefing Book,* No. 613, 12 December 2017.

Though it has often been presented since as a response to a 'Russian threat', NATO expansion was entirely premised on Russian weakness. As James Goldgeier put it in his 1999 book on NATO enlargement, *Not Whether But When*, 'the possibility that Poland or the Czech Republic would actually need defending seemed remote'.[18] The USSR's implosion and the ensuing traumas of transition instead allowed the West to move into the strategic vacuum left in the region. Clinton himself pointed to this logic in December 1994, declaring at the OSCE's Budapest summit that 'we must not allow the Iron Curtain to be replaced by a veil of indifference. We must not consign new democracies to a grey zone'.[19] That May, former national security adviser Zbigniew Brzezinski had called for 'the potentially destabilizing geopolitical no man's land between Russia and the European Union' to be 'promptly fill[ed]'.[20] During the Cold War, the two sides had been separated across much of Europe's breadth by unaffiliated or neutral countries, from Finland and Sweden through Austria and down to Yugoslavia. After 1991, no such buffer zone was necessary.

The fact that NATO expansion could be disconnected from any actual military risks no doubt smoothed its way among policy-making elites in Washington. There was, to be sure, opposition from prominent figures: George Kennan, the original architect of 'containment', called it a 'fateful error'; Thomas Friedman, holding forth in the pages of the *New York Times*, worried it would imperil efforts to prevent nuclear proliferation.[21] There were concerns, too, that overly aggressive moves by the US to benefit from Russia's weakness now might produce a backlash there later – that a punitive post-Soviet Versailles settlement might produce a revanchist Russian nationalism. Yet these considerations were overpowered by two other motivations. One was precisely the chance to wrest Eastern Europe out of Moscow's orbit for good. Unlikely to come around again, it was simply too good an opportunity to pass up – especially since many of the new governments in Eastern Europe were themselves keen to join.

The other was a deep suspicion of Russia among Western policy-making elites, dating back through the Cold War all the way to 1917. The Bolshevik Revolution had created a breach in the international state system, a hole in the map that no amount of diplomacy or *détente* had been able to close. The fall of Communism, although it brought down the capitalist West's systemic rival, didn't fully close it either – leaving in place a fundamental mistrust of Moscow in Washington and other Western capitals. (This might be termed a 'White legacy', in contrast to the 'Red bequests' discussed earlier.) As long as Yeltsin was in power and willing to fall in with Western thinking, these doubts could be assuaged. But the moment things changed, the older ideological reflex would kick in once more, fuelling criticisms of Russia that the West never levelled at far more repressive regimes whose interests were more compatible with Western aims, such as those in Saudi Arabia or Egypt, say. NATO expansion was therefore to some extent an insurance policy against an outcome that, ironically, the expansion would ultimately help to create: the return to the world stage of an independent Russia, with interests distinct from those of the West.

In the early 1990s, though, such a prospect remained distant. The immediate strategic gains from NATO expansion were clear enough that a bipartisan consensus soon developed around the policy in the US. However, the Clinton administration also knew that too rapid an expansion would torpedo Yeltsin's chances of re-election, so from 1993 to 1996 it pursued a two-track policy, offering Russia and other Eastern European states membership in a 'Partnership for Peace' that seemed to be an alternative to an expanded NATO. (Yeltsin was certainly taken in by the ruse: 'This is a brilliant idea, it is a stroke of genius!' he exclaimed to US secretary of state Warren Christopher, adding: 'Tell Bill I am thrilled.')[22] Meanwhile the US prepared the ground for a first round of NATO enlargement – starting in 1994 with the NATO Enlargement Facilitation Act, designed to smooth the path of Poland, Hungary and the Czech Republic to join the alliance.

This dual-track approach struck hard-line Cold Warriors as needless pandering to the Russians; Henry Kissinger apparently asked, 'Whoever heard of a military alliance begging with a weakened adversary?'[23] But it was in any case abandoned soon enough. Once Yeltsin was safely re-installed in the Kremlin, in the summer of 1996 – in no small measure thanks to covert assistance from the West[24] – the US could be more blunt. Clinton's deputy secretary of state (and former college roommate), Strobe Talbott, told Anatoly Chubais, chief of Yeltsin's presidential administration, 'that NATO enlargement was going to happen, and . . . that Russia had to make sure that it did not look like Moscow had lost'.[25]

In March 1999, when Hungary, the Czech Republic and Poland formally joined the alliance, NATO immediately moved ahead with a second wave of expansion, establishing 'Membership Action Plans' for nine more countries, including the three Baltic states. Both of these developments took place at the height of the NATO intervention in Kosovo – conducted without UN Security Council authorization, since it was evident that Russia would veto it – underscoring still more deeply Russia's irrelevance on the world stage. Primakov, then prime minister, was on his way to Washington when the bombing of Yugoslavia started, and ordered his plane to turn around in protest. It was a forceful symbolic gesture – but then, Russia's means were too limited to do much else.

Washington's ability to impose its will on the question of NATO enlargement, whatever Moscow's objections, made plain the fundamental imbalance in power between the two countries. Hard enough in itself for Russia to accept, it was made still worse by the manner in which US diplomats wielded their authority. As early as 1993, Kozyrev – who could scarcely be accused of hostility to the West – was protesting to Talbott, 'It's bad enough having you people tell us what you're going to do whether we like it or not. Don't add insult to injury by also telling us that it's in our interests to obey your orders.' Talbott's assistant at the time, Victoria Nuland – who later became infamous for her role, captured in an

intercepted phone call, in choosing Ukraine's post-Maidan government – apparently observed that this was 'what happens when
you try to get the Russians to eat their spinach'.[26] The condescen-
sion behind such words – the infantilization of what was, after all,
a state with almost half the world's nuclear weapons – would have
been only too apparent to Washington's Russian interlocutors.

The drive for NATO expansion also made it clear that there was
no room for Russia within European institutions or Euro-Atlantic
security arrangements. The Yeltsin government several times
floated the idea of joining NATO, but Russian membership was
never seriously considered. Despite its weakness in the 1990s,
Russia was still too large and powerful a state to be easily fitted
into the system as it was. According to Brzezinski, 'the politically
decisive fact is that Russia bulks too large, is too backward currently
and too powerful potentially to be assimilated as simply yet
another member of the European Union or NATO. It would
dilute the Western character of the European community and the
American preponderance within the alliance.'[27] As part of NATO
or an expanded EU, for example, it would have been on a par with
Germany or France in terms of its decision-making influence,
capable of banding together with either to block US designs.

The whole course of US policy toward Europe in that decade
was precisely geared to averting such a scenario. The 'Partnership
for Peace', the Permanent Joint Council set up in 1997, and the
NATO–Russia Council that replaced the PJC in 2002 may have
seemed to provide avenues for co-operation between Moscow
and the West. But as the Russians quickly realized, these were
substitutes for membership rather than stepping-stones to it.
When Putin, installed as president just weeks earlier, asked
Clinton at a June 2000 summit how he would respond to Russia's
joining NATO, Clinton apparently looked desperately at the
advisers flanking him: Secretary of State Madeleine Albright,
who 'pretended that she was looking at a fly on the wall', and
National Security Adviser Sandy Berger, who 'did not react at all'.

Clinton was reduced to saying he would 'personally' – a word he repeated three times, to be on the safe side – support it.[28] But since he would be leaving office a few months later, this assurance was not worth much.

The process of NATO enlargement is crucial to understanding why and how relations between Russia and the West later deteriorated. It demonstrated the basic imbalance that has governed strategic calculations on both sides ever since: the US enjoyed accumulated advantages that enabled it either to attend to or ignore Russian interests as it pleased, while Russia retained enough of its great-power habits of mind to resent this state of affairs, but lacked the capacity fundamentally to alter it. Yet although this resentment increased over the next decade, the underlying thrust of Russian policy remained broadly oriented toward the West. This contradictory dynamic, in which Russia's aspiration to join the West mingled with rejection of it, underpinned the mounting confrontations between the Kremlin and Western governments from the mid-2000s onward.

Amid the steady worsening of relations between Russia and the West in recent years, Putin has increasingly been depicted in the Western media as their countries' sworn enemy, steadfastly opposed to liberal democracy and bent on undermining it from without. But it's worth recalling that for most of the time he has been in power, the West – and in particular Europe – has been the lodestar of Russia's foreign-policy thinking. To begin with, Putin seemed to represent a return to the 'Westernizing' tendency abandoned by Primakov. Shortly before assuming the presidency for the first time in 2000, Putin told David Frost he sought 'more profound' integration with NATO, and 'would not rule out' Russian membership.[29] Around the same time, in the biographical interviews that made up *First Person*, he described Russians as 'a part of the Western European culture. No matter where our people live, in the far East or in the south, we are Europeans.'[30]

Putin's points of reference were European even when they weren't at all flattering: at the end of 1999, he said that it would take fifteen years of rapid growth for Russia to draw level with Portugal's current per capita GDP.[31] (Russia reached that milestone in 2011; but by then Portugal was further ahead, and even amid the deep recession sparked by the eurozone crisis, its GDP per capita was still more than one and a half times that of Russia.) At the start of the twenty-first century, then, the Kremlin still envisaged a future of co-operation and ultimate economic convergence with the West. The sharp disagreements over Kosovo in 1999 were, for the time being, seen as a passing anomaly rather than the basis for a widening breach.

The 11 September attacks prompted a shift in Russia's policy stance. Putin had insistently framed his war on Chechnya, launched in 1999, as part of a wider struggle against 'Islamic extremism'.[32] In the aftermath of the Twin Towers' destruction, he saw the potential for an alliance with the Bush administration against 'terrorism', opening Russian airspace and encouraging Central Asian states to help with the assault on Afghanistan. These were startling geopolitical concessions, and they were applauded by Russia's liberals, who at the time called for Russia to line up with the West in a joint struggle against 'barbarism'. Grigory Yavlinsky and Boris Nemtsov backed the assault on Afghanistan, and the deputy leader of the Union of Right Forces' parliamentary delegation asserted that 'Russia must participate in the action of retribution'.[33]

Yet the Kremlin's hopes for a durable 'anti-terrorist' consensus came to nothing, and the co-operation between Washington and Moscow was short-lived. The former's unilateral withdrawal from the Anti-Ballistic Missile Treaty in June 2002 was an early sign that Russian overtures would not be reciprocated. The disparity built into US–Russia relations, meanwhile, became even more glaring now that the US was committed to deploying its power still more aggressively, as the 'War on Terror' morphed rapidly into a crusade to remake the Middle East. Russia joined France and Germany in voicing reservations about the US assault on Iraq. But Russia's concerns didn't stem from any attachment to international law or sympathy for Iraqi civilians – it had, after all, recently levelled what remained of Grozny, burying thousands of its own citizens under the rubble. It was, rather, alarmed at the US's unconstrained use of military force around the globe, and its deployment of that force to impose regime change.

The question of regime change became especially significant for the Kremlin in the mid-2000s. Though it had successfully neutralized opposition within the country, the 'imitation democratic' regime nonetheless remained vulnerable to pressure or even overthrow from the outside. A year after the invasion of Iraq, the accession of seven more countries to NATO brought the alliance directly to Russia's border. At the end of 2004, protests over rigged elections in Ukraine sparked the 'Orange Revolution', blocking Moscow's preferred candidate, Viktor Yanukovych, and ultimately bringing his pro-Western opponent, Viktor Yushchenko, to power instead. Greeted in the West as a democratic flowering, but seen in the Kremlin as the product of Western machinations, the Ukraine crisis of 2004–05 was crucially different from the previous 'Colour Revolutions' in Serbia (2000) and Georgia (2003). There was much more at stake for Russia than in those previous cases: the Kremlin had poured a great deal of money and effort into securing the presidency for Yanukovych, and the geopolitical outcomes of his defeat were far more serious – potentially opening the way for NATO to emplace itself along almost all of Russia's western borders.

In the case of Ukraine, moreover, external strategic issues were intertwined with internal political questions. The 'Orange Revolution' represented a frontal challenge to Russia's own 'imitation democratic' regime, raising the possibility that popular energies – till now excluded from the business of government across the post-Soviet space – might surge back once more, as in 1989–91, to threaten the existing system. The examples of Georgia and Ukraine proved contagious: Kyrgyzstan's 'Tulip Revolution' followed in early 2005, while comparable though unsuccessful movements emerged elsewhere (Azerbaijan, Belarus, Mongolia). From 2004–05 onward, the defence of what the Kremlin saw as Russia's interests abroad became inseparable from the impulse for self-preservation at home, tying Russian foreign policy ever more closely to concerns over domestic order.

Yet even amid growing tensions over Iraq, NATO expansion and Ukraine, Moscow's foreign-policy stance was still founded on a sense of commonalities with the West. In an April 2005 speech to both houses of the Russian parliament, Putin said that 'Russia was, is and will, of course, be a major European power', and spoke of shared 'ideals of freedom, human rights, justice and democracy'.[34] At the same time, there was a new insistence on the country's capacity to determine its own future. In the same speech Putin asserted that, 'as a sovereign nation, Russia can and will decide for itself the timeframe and conditions for its progress' along the road to 'freedom and democracy'. In effect, Putin had combined the 'Westernizing' and 'statist' lines of Russian foreign-policy thinking.

But this synthesis was inherently unstable, expressing a desire for alliance with the West while asserting independence from it. The contradiction was apparent in Putin's February 2007 address to the Munich Security Conference, where he laid out a litany of complaints about Western behaviour, focusing especially on Iraq and NATO expansion but embracing a great many other themes, from nuclear proliferation to the WTO. Though this was widely interpreted by the mainstream media as an outburst of angry anti-Western sentiment, it makes more sense to see it as a fit of frustration – which had built up precisely because Russia's attempts to forge a pragmatic alliance with the West, and to develop closer trade and economic ties, kept failing.

The continued failure to gain better access to the EU's markets was a particular sore point for Russia. From the 1990s until the global economic crisis of 2008, EU states had accounted for around two-thirds of the country's imports and exports, and even after that, as Russia laboured under a downturn and then the pressure of the 2014 Western sanctions, they still accounted for about half.[35] But a string of Russia–EU summits – in Samara in 2007, Khanti-Mansiisk in 2008, Khabarovsk in 2009 – did not produce any substantive agreements.

Nonetheless, the ideal of Russian integration into some broader, 'Greater European' arrangement persisted. In June 2008, for example, the newly installed President Dmitri Medvedev – much more of a liberal Westernizer than Putin – put forward the concept of a 'Euro-Atlantic space' stretching 'from Vancouver to Vladivostok'.[36] The idea applied to security questions as well as economic ones: Medvedev also proposed a new 'all-European' security architecture, apparently whipping out his iPad to discuss it at the 2010 Moscow session of the Munich Security Conference.[37] Posited as an alternative to the Atlanticist structures of NATO, the concept would have required European states to voluntarily peel away from the US. There was little interest in the scheme outside Moscow, but just to be sure, NATO chief Anders Fogh Rasmussen pointed out in late 2009 that 'we do have a framework already', while Secretary of State Hillary Clinton reinforced the message early in 2010 by explaining that the US's and Russia's 'common goals are best pursued in the context of existing institutions, such as the OSCE and the NATO–Russia Council, rather than by negotiating new treaties, as Russia has suggested – a very long and cumbersome process'.[38] NATO would not be dislodged as the sole security bloc in the Euro-Atlantic area, and Russia would remain outside it.

Between the spring and summer of 2008, Russian–Western relations moved swiftly from rhetorical stand-offs to proxy war. In February, Kosovo's declaration of independence was swiftly recognized by the US and other leading NATO states, setting a precedent Russia deemed alarming. In April, a NATO summit in Bucharest raised the prospect of membership for Georgia and

Ukraine – only to defer it until some unspecified future date, in the face of Putin's strenuous objections. Meanwhile tensions were escalating in the breakaway Georgian regions of Abkhazia and South Ossetia, de facto Russian protectorates since brief separatist wars in the early 1990s. In early August 2008, Georgian President Mikheil Saakashvili – seemingly with encouragement from the US – suddenly moved to recapture South Ossetia, providing Russia with a ready pretext for armed intervention.

Militarily, the conflict was a mismatch, and was over after five days of fighting. Politically, it was far more consequential. It was partly a kind of retaliation on the plane of international law for previous Western actions: Medvedev invoked the West's own doctrines of 'humanitarian intervention' and the 'responsibility to protect' ('R2P'), as deployed in Kosovo in 1999 and agreed at the UN's 2005 World Summit, respectively. In the immediate aftermath of the war, moreover, the Kremlin recognized South Ossetia and Abkhazia as independent states, citing the barely six-month-old precedent of Kosovo. The staggering hypocrisy of this gesture, from a government that had fought two wars to prevent Chechen independence, hardly needs emphasizing. But the Georgian operation was more immediately intended to call the West's bluff on further NATO enlargement, effectively asking if it was willing to start a full-scale global war for the sake of tiny Georgia. The answer, despite much bluster from US Republicans such as John McCain, was no. Behind this confrontation, meanwhile, the issue of Ukraine – strategically far more significant to both Russia and the West – lurked in the background, as an obvious future flashpoint.

In March 2009, Secretary of State Clinton presented her Russian counterpart, Sergei Lavrov, with a yellow plastic box featuring a red button marked 'reset' in English – a tacky token of the Obama administration's desire to improve US–Russian relations in the wake of the Russo-Georgian War. But the State Department had made a basic translation error when labelling the button in Russian: instead of *perezagruzka* it read *peregruzka* – not 'reset', but 'overload'. The gaffe pointed to an embarrassing lack of either competence or care in Washington; it was also an unbeatably Freudian summary of the whole trajectory of post-Cold War relations between the two countries.

The arrival of the Obama administration was meant to herald a new phase of co-operation, but brought the exact opposite: a period of increasing antagonism and mutual suspicion. In the West, the reasons for this are often sought in Putin's authoritarian persona, or in a broader Russian nostalgia for superpower status. But while both these factors were certainly present, neither was as important as the underlying dynamic of Western–Russian relations, which remained unaltered by the empty diplomatic gestures of the 'reset'. Moscow's aspirations for alliance or integration were repeatedly ignored or rebuffed by the West, which had its own plans and priorities. Foremost among these was the drive by NATO and the EU to bring the former Soviet and Warsaw Pact states of Eastern Europe into the Western orbit, reformatting their political and economic systems along liberal capitalist lines. For much of the 1990s and 2000s, Russia was powerless to prevent the advance of this project. But enforced passivity should not have been mistaken for willing acceptance. What has happened over the past decade, far from being an unforeseen escalation of tensions, is a collision – delayed or masked for a time – of incompatible interests.

Russia's actions on the world stage over the past few years have been marked by a rising rhetorical aggression, and by an increased adventurism in practice: the annexation of Crimea and support for rebels in the Donbass; intervention in Syria; courting of hard-right candidates and movements campaigning against the established order in major Western states, from Trump in the US to Le Pen in France and the Alternativ für Deutschland party in Germany. These moves have often been interpreted as being all of

a piece, as parts of some deliberate Kremlin design for a conservative world order that would overturn the dominance of liberal
democratic norms. Russia's rulers have indeed come to see themselves as fundamentally opposed to the Western liberal-democratic
order, and have increasingly embraced a set of geopolitical ideas
that emphasize the country's peculiar 'Eurasian' destiny. But we
should avoid the temptation to explain these developments as
being driven by a coherent, pre-established agenda. Russia's decisions have been shaped most decisively by the geopolitical
environment in which the country has to operate, and this environment is dominated by other powers – the US above all.

Most of Russia's conduct on the world stage, in fact, has to be
seen as a series of responses to this overriding constraint. Since
the Ukraine crisis, those responses have been increasingly combative; but they have also been largely improvised, focused on
short-term tactical thinking rather than any longer-term project.
The apparent aggression stems not from a growing confidence or
sense of purpose, but from a pervasive and deepening anxiety
about Russian weakness. It is this that fuelled the Putin administration's attempts to reassert Russia's global relevance – and, first
of all, to reverse the setbacks it suffered in Ukraine.

The Ukraine crisis looms large in any account of recent relations between Russia and the West, for obvious reasons – it was
the annexation of Crimea that first prompted the West to institute
sanctions against Russia in 2014 – and less immediately apparent
ones. Beneath the turmoil of events, the battle for Ukraine also
exposed, and at the same time exacerbated, the dynamics that have
shaped relations between Russia and the West since the end of the
Cold War. Firstly, it confirmed Russia's steady loss of influence
over the former states of the USSR. In one realm after another,
Moscow's capacity to secure favourable outcomes in the region has
diminished to historic lows. The Orange Revolution of 2004–05
and the toppling of Yanukovych in 2014 were the most humiliating political reversals, but there were others. In tiny Abkhazia, for

instance, the very fact of Kremlin support led voters to reject Moscow's preferred presidential candidate in 2004. And Russian attempts to establish a post-Soviet security architecture have met with uneven success. Four of the CIS states withdrew from its Collective Security Treaty to set up their own organization in 1999, named 'GUAM' after their initials (Georgia, Ukraine, Azerbaijan and Moldova). Meanwhile the Collective Security Treaty Organization, founded in 2002 and intended as a kind of Eurasian NATO – its members are Armenia, Belarus, Kazakhstan, Kyrgyzstan, Russia and Tajikistan – has so far been little more than a pretext for summitry.

Kremlin projects for economic integration – the Eurasian Economic Community and its 2014 successor, the Eurasian Economic Union – have fared little better. This is largely because there has been a rapid diversification of trade patterns across the former USSR: by 2009, barely 15 per cent of Russia's trade was with CIS countries, and only two of those countries – Belarus and Ukraine – were among Russia's top ten trading partners. Conversely, only 15 per cent of CIS countries' imports came from Russia.[39] For both Russia and its neighbours, the EU was now the main partner, accounting for about half of imports and exports in each case. In effect, the disintegration of the USSR into separate political units had segued into a geopolitical and economic dispersal.

Secondly, the Ukraine crisis made clear once again the enormous disparity in power and resources between Russia and the West. In the 1990s, the prime movers in Western policy toward Eastern Europe and the former USSR had been the US and NATO, but in the 2000s it was more often the EU that drove it. In 2004, Brussels launched its 'European Neighbourhood Project', which called for structural reforms in adjoining countries in exchange for improved market access, an easing of visa restrictions, and financial assistance packages totalling $16 billion for 2007–2013.[40] Initially targeted at the former Soviet states bordering the countries that had just joined the EU, the programme was soon expanded to include countries on the southern and eastern shores of the Mediterranean.

In 2009, the EU launched another initiative, the 'Eastern Partnership', which was more specifically designed to pull the former Soviet republics into its domain. The aim, as expressed at the Prague Summit that May, was 'to create the necessary conditions to accelerate political association and further economic integration between the European Union and interested partner countries'.[41] 'Action plans', specifying concrete measures to be taken and standards to be met across a whole range of economic sectors and areas of government, were developed for Armenia, Azerbaijan, Belarus, Georgia, Moldova and Ukraine. At the same time, the EU began negotiations with each of these states over Association Agreements and what the EU called Deep and Comprehensive Free Trade Areas (DCFTAs).

Yet there was more to these agreements than just trade: they were also designed to bring about these countries' alignment – or 'higher convergence', as the Association Agreement with Ukraine put it – with the EU's European Security and Defence Policy, including greater military and technical co-operation with EU states. Though falling far short of actual EU membership, these Agreements were clearly an attempt to lock the former Soviet countries of Eastern Europe into the EU's sphere of influence – and lock them out of Russia's.

It was, of course, Yanukovych's abrupt U-turn on the EU Association Agreement that sparked the Maidan protests in late 2013. Ukraine seemed to be caught in a choice between the EU's free-trade agreement and the Kremlin's project for a Eurasian Customs Union – a choice often framed by Maidan supporters in civilizational terms, as being between 'Europe' and 'Asia', between a modernizing European destiny and the backwardness of the Soviet past. Yet there were many other factors behind Yanukovych's decision – not least a concern over the potential impact of free trade on an economy already reeling under the impact of

IMF-decreed budgetary austerity. The manufacturing and extractive industries of Eastern Ukraine stood to lose a great deal from
the DCFTA. Conversely, many Western Ukrainians desperately
wanted legal paths for labour migration to EU countries, where
wages were significantly higher.[42] These divergent socio-economic
interests often mapped onto other kinds of internal difference in
Ukraine, generating significant public support for both the
'Europeanist' and 'Russian' alternatives. But there were huge asym-
metries in the power and resources of the two.

Despite the Kremlin's mounting concern over the prospect of
Ukraine joining NATO and becoming more closely integrated
with the EU, it was unable to make Kiev a genuinely better offer.
Putin's plan to buy $15 billion of government debt and give
Ukraine deep discounts on gas came too late to help Yanukovych,
but it wouldn't have made much difference if it had been offered
earlier. Russia simply could not match the West's combined
economic and ideological appeal.

Just as important, Russia also lacked the power to persuade the
West not to absorb Ukraine into its sphere of influence. The
aggressiveness of the Kremlin's response to the Maidan protests
was in part driven by fear that their example would encourage
protesters at home. But Russia's words and deeds were at the same
time very much aimed at the West. Prior to Yanukovych's fall,
Russia sought to delay as long as possible the arrival of an unambiguously pro-Western government in Kiev. After his removal
from power in February 2014, the Kremlin lost its political leverage there. Its subsequent moves – annexation of Crimea, support
for armed separatists in the Donbass – were first and foremost
attempts to shake the West's tightening grip on Ukraine. If significant portions of the country were turned into either war zones or
contested territories, perhaps the EU and NATO would think
twice about offering Ukraine membership. But despite the
Kremlin's references at the time to 'Novorossiia' – the old tsarist
name for the lands along the Black Sea's northern shore, hinting at

a potential claim to more of Ukraine's territory – these actions were tactical improvisations rather than part of a long-held plan to dismember Ukraine. The Kremlin was in effect frantically drawing one line in the sand after another, lines the West kept blithely ignoring. The rapid escalation of Russia's response and the very crudity of its methods were in themselves a measure of the asymmetry of power between it and the West.

The same is true of the triumphalist sloganeering that followed the annexation of Crimea. Russian state media depicted it as a patriotic feat, reuniting the motherland with what Putin, in his March 2014 speech requesting the peninsula's formal admission to the Russian Federation, called 'an inseparable part of Russia'. (In the same speech, Putin notably reiterated many of his criticisms of Western double standards, and again angrily cited the example of Kosovo.)[43] Western governments and media, meanwhile, furiously protested the annexation. US secretary of state John Kerry called it 'an incredible act of aggression', adding – with the straightest of faces – 'You just don't in the twenty-first century behave in nineteenth-century fashion by invading another country on [a] completely trumped-up pretext.'[44]

This trading of rhetorical blows cannot obscure the fact that the actual consequences of the Crimean annexation were much to the West's benefit and to Russia's disadvantage. It accelerated Ukraine's flight out of Russia's sphere of influence: public support for NATO membership increased in Ukraine, and military ties between NATO and the Ukrainian armed forces were strengthened, bringing the alliance still closer to Russia's heartland; meanwhile, a DCFTA between Ukraine and the EU came into force in 2016, setting the country on a path to economic integration with Europe rather than with Russia. At the same time, the fallout from the Ukraine crisis brought sanctions that damaged Russia's economy – cutting off much-needed international investment, for example – and deepened its international isolation. By 2017 the Russian economy had begun to recover somewhat, thanks to a

rise in global oil prices and the stimulus given to domestic production by the sanctions' stifling of imports. But there can be no
question that events in Ukraine after 2013 added up to a significant geopolitical defeat for Putin.

This is the context in which Russia's subsequent foreign-policy
moves need to be understood. The intervention in Syria, launched
in September 2015, was in large measure a response to the disaster
of the Kremlin's policy in Ukraine. There were, to be sure, many
motivations behind the decision to deepen Russia's involvement in
the Syrian conflict – a war in which it was already implicated
through its support for the Assad regime. But some of the factors
most commonly invoked were by 2015 secondary to Russia's most
pressing foreign-policy needs.

Economic and political ties between Moscow and Damascus
stretched back to the Cold War, and might suggest an obvious
material reason for Russia to prop up Bashar al-Assad's rule. Under
Assad's father, Syria had been one of the USSR's few state-level allies
in the Middle East, and received substantial economic and military
aid in exchange for the lease of a naval base at Tartus.[45] In the 1990s,
these ties languished as Russia's economy collapsed and its foreign
policy turned it away from its former client states. In the 2000s, the
Putin government revived the Syrian connection, and in 2006
signed an arms deal worth $4 billion, and in 2010 another worth
$20 billion.[46] But with the Arab Spring and the outbreak of civil
war in Syria, whatever material stakes Russia had there rapidly dwindled: bilateral trade slumped from $1.2 billion in 2011 to $376
million two years later – a lower volume of trade than Russia had
with Iraq or Libya, and barely a tenth the size of its trade with Israel.[47]

Domestic considerations certainly played some role. The Syrian
intervention gave Putin a brief patriotic ratings boost; unlike
Russia's semi-covert role in eastern Ukraine – where its troops
operated at arm's length as 'volunteers' – this one could be loudly

claimed, and broadcast on national television, though its popularity dwindled soon enough. The Russian military and its arms manufacturers also stood to gain. The 2008 war with Georgia had, among other things, revealed how far behind Russia was in terms of technology and military organization, prompting a major overhaul and upgrading of weapons. Syria, already devastated by years of war, provided a testing ground – and showroom – for the new-look armed forces and weapons systems. Among the main buyers in the region were Algeria and Egypt, who in 2014 signed arms deals with Russia worth \$2.7 billion and \$3.5 billion respectively.[48]

In one important sense, internal concerns overlapped with external ones. Moscow's bid to ensure Assad's survival in power was to some degree motivated by its aversion to regime change. A deep legitimism had been built into Russian policy since the Orange Revolution in Ukraine; the Maidan increased the feeling of urgency behind it. The same pro-incumbent logic applied to the Middle East during the Arab Spring: the Kremlin came to view the revolts as another iteration of the 'Colour Revolutions', encouraged if not actually sponsored by the US and its allies. It did not immediately see the 2011 revolts in Tunisia and Egypt as conforming to a larger pattern; it was only the fall of Gaddafi that really fixed this interpretation in the Kremlin's mind. In March 2011, when the UN Security Council voted on a resolution authorizing no-fly zones over Libya, President Medvedev decided to abstain rather than veto it – a gesture that signalled the persistence of the pro-Western current in Russian foreign-policy thinking, and opened the way for a Western intervention that replicated the destruction and turmoil visited on Iraq. When a similar fate threatened Assad, Moscow was determined not to make the same mistakes, and vetoed eleven UNSC resolutions on Syria between October 2011 and April 2018.

Russia's intervention in Syria, starting in 2015, was initially underpinned by the same anti-regime change logic, which lent its actions a brutal simplicity. The complexity of the conflict – the range of political identities within the rebellion, the country's regional and sectarian mosaic – was reduced to a struggle between Assad and a monolithic opposition that Moscow, too, labelled 'terrorists'. On the battlefield, all anti-Assad forces were placed in the same category as ISIS. This may have made Russia's stance more coherent than that of Western powers, in which different Western allies – or even different agencies of the same government – backed opposing militias.[49] But it was scarcely less destructive, as the fate of Aleppo demonstrated. The target of ferocious bombing since 2012, the city was subjected to further pounding by Russian airstrikes in 2015 and 2016. At the same time, however, Russia's defence of Assad was not unreserved or especially entrenched. Only weeks after launching airstrikes to prevent the Syrian government from falling, the Russian Foreign Ministry's spokesperson was asserting that Assad's continuation in power was 'absolutely not' a matter of principle for Moscow; its professed concern was that regime change should not be imposed from without, and that Syrian state institutions should remain intact during any political transition.[50]

But the central aim of the Kremlin's intervention in Syria was, in my view, neither to protect Assad nor to prevent regime change per se; it was, rather, an attempt to re-establish Russia's importance on the world stage. A desire for more equal treatment from the West had been a longstanding theme of Russian diplomacy, from Primakov onward, and it recurred in disagreements over Syria. In February 2013, for instance, Russian Foreign Minister Sergei Lavrov told a TV interviewer that the US 'needs to be taught that affairs can only be conducted on the basis of equality, balance of interests and mutual respect'.[51] After the Maidan, and with the US and its allies bent on a policy of isolating Russia internationally, the urge to claim parity gave way to a more pressing need to reassert Russia's relevance.

Syria became the critical means for doing so. Already in September 2013, Russia had given notice of its diplomatic capacities, brokering a deal designed to destroy Syria's chemical weapons arsenal and thus avert the airstrikes the Obama administration had threatened against Assad. Further waves of diplomatic activity around Syria followed, including hosting meetings of Syrian opposition groups and the Assad government in Moscow in January 2015. Even when Russia began its own armed intervention in Syria a few months later, the Kremlin was not entirely switching from the diplomatic track – further talks took place in Vienna in October 2015, at the same time as Russian airstrikes were being carried out. Rather, the military action in Syria was evidently calibrated to show that Russia could materially affect the course of the conflict – and was therefore a power whose interests had to be taken into account, rather than a pariah facing ever deeper isolation.

The same aspiration, too, explains the revival, a decade and a half after 11 September 2001, of Putin's dream of an international anti-terrorist alliance, which he put forward to the UN General Assembly in September 2015. A grand US–Russian coalition of this kind would no doubt have levelled what was left of Syria, jointly creating a desert and calling it peace. The idea was never likely to be endorsed by a Democratic administration, and although it seemed during the 2016 campaign as if Trump might be amenable to the idea, that hope quickly evaporated after November amid the constant stream of allegations of Russian election meddling.

With Trump's victory, Russia moved to the centre of US public and media debate as never before in the post-Soviet era. Among dismayed Democrats, Russian interference became the default explanation for Clinton's defeat: it was as if the Kremlin had hacked American democracy itself. Of course, whatever trouble the Russian government may have wanted to cause the Clinton campaign, it made little difference to the actual outcome of the vote. (And all indications are that the Kremlin, like so many other observers, expected Clinton to win anyway.) But 'Russia' quickly became a convenient, all-purpose signifier enabling many

American liberals to avoid discussing the multiple factors behind Trump's disastrous success, from the anti-democratic distortions of the electoral college system to the disenfranchisement of voters, especially African-Americans, through voter ID laws and mass incarceration. Rather than confront the deep flaws in the US's own institutions, political system and society that produced the freak result, for many it was more convenient – more emotionally accurate, too – to blame Trump's ascent on an outside power, and implicitly to identify Trump himself as a foreign body.

Even before Trump's inauguration, it became clear that tarring the new president by association with Russia would be the predominant angle of attack for much of the US media and political establishment. In January 2017, several intelligence agencies signed on to an extremely thin and barely literate 'assessment' that 'Vladimir Putin ordered an influence campaign in 2016 aimed at the US presidential election'.[52] For months thereafter, one figure in the Trump administration after another was found to have suspicious ties to Russia: Secretary of State Rex Tillerson was too cosy with Putin, national security adviser Michael Flynn took money for lobbying efforts, Attorney General Jeff Sessions lied about his meetings with the Russian ambassador to the US, Trump's son Donald Jr and other members of his campaign team discussed with assorted Russians how to damage Clinton, and so on.

Much of this was undoubtedly murky, though crookedness and lying of this kind are hardly unusual fare in US politics. The difference lay in the brazenness of the Trump campaign, and the fact that it was connected to Russia – now recurrently referred to as a 'hostile power'. Not just corruption, then, but also treason was in the air. The paranoias of the Cold War seemed to have made a comeback: in November 2016, for example, a mysterious online group called PropOrNot went full McCarthy by releasing 'The List', designed to name and shame – or indeed casually smear – websites that it believed 'reliably echo Russian propaganda'. In September 2017, a new entity called the Committee to Investigate Russia released a video in which Morgan Freeman told viewers, 'We have been attacked. We are at war.' More than the 2016 election was at stake: Putin and his army of hackers had made Americans 'distrust their media, their political processes, even their neighbours'.

'Russia' became what Masha Gessen called 'the universal rhetorical weapon of American politics'.[53] But what was the connection between 'Russia' as deployed within the US political scene and Russia itself? The main concerns of those resorting to 'Russia' as a rhetorical weapon were domestic, focused on undermining the Trump presidency and, if possible, levering him out of office. Yet the Russia panic had real consequences on the international stage: it made impossible any easing of the sanctions regime, and blocked off for the foreseeable future any rapprochement with Moscow. The possibility of a new bargain with the West, which the Putin administration evidently hoped to secure under Trump, all but vanished.

The accumulated tensions of the previous decade are unlikely to dissipate any time soon. But does this mean that we do indeed find ourselves living through a 'New Cold War'? To some extent, the very idea of a cold war is a kind of geopolitical speech act: if enough people in power decide they are in one, it will materialize. Yet there are decisive differences between current frictions and the global contest that followed the Second World War. Most obvious is the lack of remotely comparable ideological stakes: it is not two rival socio-economic systems that now confront each other, but states, or blocs of them, with opposed interests. Then there is the fact that Russia–West tensions have not so far dragged in the same array of allies and clients as before: this time around, China, East and South Asia, Africa and Latin America are all bystanders. For the same reason, the struggle this time is much more geographically circumscribed; with the grim exception of Syria, the zones of contention have been in Eastern Europe. Overall, both Russia and the world have been so transformed over the past generation that none of the Cold War conditions can be said to apply.

Why, then, has the Cold War framework proved so tempting as a means of understanding relations between Russia and the West? For hardened hawks and Beltway pundits it no doubt offers the comfort of familiarity, as well as a ready repertoire of tropes and imagery. But it has gained momentum among a wider public, both in the US and far beyond its borders. The idea of a 'New Cold War' seems, more than anything, designed to fill a conceptual vacuum – compensating for the lack, in the minds of many, of ways to grasp the disconcerting novelty of the current geopolitical moment.

Taken together, the developments of the past few years confirmed that the world had entered a new geopolitical era. These events marked both the demise of the fantasy of Russian integration or alliance with the West, and a durable shift to a more confrontational stance. Again, this was not the result of a pre-programmed Russian hostility to Western values, or indeed to Western policy goals more broadly: Russia has, after all, lined up with the US several times on key issues, such as sanctions on North Korea and Iran, and has made sure to coordinate its airstrikes on Syria with the USAF, for example. But where US and Russian interests diverge most sharply, the Kremlin has sought to counteract or forestall Western moves more actively than before.

Still, it should be borne in mind that in the cases of Ukraine, Syria and the 2016 US presidential election, the Kremlin's actions were tactical improvisations rather than moves in any alternative grand strategy. The suddenness and decisiveness of these actions seemed almost an end in themselves, designed to alter the parameters of the geopolitical situation so radically and abruptly that the West would be compelled to change course. The problem with this approach, however, was that after each dramatic move, the situation began to settle once more into its normal pattern, creating the need for another, still more drastic move; the result was that Russian policy was gradually replaced by a string of increasingly risky *fuites en avant*.

The Syrian intervention was in other respects a more significant moment than the Kremlin perhaps intended. It was Moscow's first serious military deployment beyond the former USSR since Afghanistan in the 1980s, other than Kosovo and small contributions to UN peacekeeping contingents; it was also the first time Russia had relied almost exclusively on the use of air power (in that regard, following very much in the US's footsteps). These were no small additions to Russia's tactical repertoire, and they set precedents that cannot be ignored or easily revoked. Once used, the methods of war have a way of generating their own reasons, until they become normalized instruments of policy – as the example of the US itself, engaged in multiple unwinnable wars disguised as limited, 'surgical' interventions, shows.

We are likely, then, to see more turbulent, unpredictable times ahead where Russia and the West are concerned – something much less stable and well-defined than a 'New Cold War'. The shift is especially striking because the underlying parameters governing relations between the two sides remain substantively unchanged: there is still, after all, a dramatic imbalance of power. The US enjoys accumulated advantages that allow it to either attend to or ignore Russian interests as it pleases. Russia, meanwhile, retains enough of its great-power habits of mind to resent this state of affairs, but cannot by itself reshape the relation of forces. Unless and until these conditions are altered, under the current logic of confrontation, more clashes are likely.

Yet something has undeniably changed. For much of the post-Soviet period, the problem of Russia's global position – both in a literal, geographical sense and in strategic terms – was largely bracketed, obscured by the lingering dream of a Westernizing Russia joining with its former adversaries. All through the gradual process of disenchantment that has taken place over the past two decades, that problem remained fundamentally unresolved. Events since the Ukraine crisis have brought us back to it, demanding that we think again about Russia's place in the world.

CHAPTER 6

Russia in the World

A SEA CHANGE HAS TAKEN place in the international order. Two and a half decades after the end of the Cold War, Russia's fantasy of integration or alliance with the West has finally been buried. It is, of course, possible that there will be some rapprochement with the West in future, and that relations will improve from their current abysmal state – particularly in Europe, where trade links and physical proximity may ultimately encourage a softening of the sanctions regime. But even then, there will be no return to the integrationist dream on Russia's part. The ground has fundamentally shifted, and from where everyone is now standing, the world looks very different.

The change in official thinking is clear enough. The Russian government's official 'foreign policy concept' from February 2013 described the country as 'an integral and inseparable part of European civilization', and made it clear that priority was to be given 'to relations with the Euro-Atlantic states which, besides geography, economy and history, have common deep-rooted civilizational ties with Russia'. In the next iteration of that document, in December 2016, these allusions had disappeared. After a long interregnum, Russia once again finds itself part of the non-West.

Yet this development has by no means resolved the much larger question of Russia's role on the global stage. If anything, it has deepened the dilemmas the country faces. What place will Russia occupy in the twenty-first-century interstate system? Will it slide down the pecking order to become a merely 'regional power', as Obama rather disparagingly put it in 2014, or will it regain its Soviet-era status as one of a handful of major global players? Despite the country's reduced circumstances compared with Soviet times, both its policymakers and much of its population retain the titan's worldview – yet without the globe-spanning ideology that gave meaning to its position in the twentieth-century world. In some ways, Russia's geopolitical situation today is an external version of the parallelism of old and new within its borders: no longer a superpower rival to the US, it is still unreconciled to becoming a second-rank regional actor.

Russia's awkward, intermediate status in itself generates all kinds of contradictions and tensions in the country's policy outlook. But there are many other constraints, both internal and external, which will work to shape its role in the world to come – limiting or inflecting the choices its leaders make, and putting multiple pressures on its political system. The possibilities for Russia will also greatly depend on what kind of world we are in: one still dominated for the foreseeable future by the US as a single superordinate power; a 'multipolar' one in which no one power can dominate; or one on the way to Chinese global hegemony.

In the long run, where is Russia going? Gogol famously ended the first part of *Dead Souls* with an evocation of the country as a troika racing headlong into the future, its destination unknown: 'All that exists on earth flies by, and, looking askance, other peoples and nations step aside and make way for her.'[1] The horizon for today's Russia seems narrower, the scope for such feverish ambition curtailed. But its role will remain significant, even in a century that promises serious shifts in the global balance of power. All the more reason, then, to think seriously about how the country sees its future self, and what obstacles and opportunities might lie along its path.

In Russia, the widening of the rift with the West was accompanied by a mounting interest in ideas that might allow the country to define a role for itself outside, or even in opposition to, the Western liberal order. The 2000s had already brought increasingly frequent assertions of Russian national pride, a resurgent patriotism that fed off the country's oil-fuelled return to a measure of economic prosperity. In the 2010s, such sentiments became more widespread and more strident, intensifying drastically after the Ukraine crisis. Politically, the new Russian nationalism was predominantly conservative, if not reactionary. Some variants of it harked back to Soviet-era glories, while others evoked a more distant imperial past. These nostalgias were far from identical in tone and content – there are, after all, differences between remembering victory over fascism and sighing over the good old days of feudalism – but they shared a compensatory impulse, finding some kind of redress for Russia's relatively reduced status in restorationist fantasies about the past. Yet another strand of nationalism looked to the European fascist and far-right tradition, seeking to impose a contradictory dream of ethno-racial purity on Russia's multi-ethnic territory. Each of these tendencies gained a certain amount of currency in the 2000s, without any of them becoming dominant ideologically – though some of the far-right's adherents certainly caused plenty of harm, carrying out dozens of vicious attacks on migrants and foreigners.*[2]

---

*   Russian nationalists were also almost certainly behind the 2009 killing in Moscow of lawyer Stanislav Markelov and journalist Anastasia Baburova, both anti-fascist activists. Markelov had argued against the early release of Colonel Yuri Budanov, who had been jailed in 2003 for torturing and killing a young Chechen woman; Budanov, who had become an icon for Russian nationalists, was himself shot and killed in 2011.

At the same time, the new century brought a revival of interest in a set of ideas that was avowedly supranational, and yet also profoundly nationalistic. 'Eurasianism' – the notion that Eurasia is home to a civilization distinct from its European, Asian or North American counterparts, with Russia at its core – has a long pedigree, dating back to the nineteenth century.[3] But it emerged in its most developed form in the 1920s among a group of Russian émigré intellectuals who, having fled the revolutionary turmoil of 1917, came to see the USSR as the heir to the tradition of Great Russian statehood, rather than as its destroyer. The Soviet Union was simply the new name for a space in which a distinctive fusion of European and Asiatic peoples and cultures would flourish. The Eurasianists included figures such as the linguists Nikolai Trubetskoi and Roman Jakobson, the geographer Pyotr Savitsky, the literary critic D. S. Mirsky, the historian George Vernadsky and others. Overall, they could be described as radical conservatives: they rejected the White exiles' nostalgia for the tsarist system, and were opposed to the crude ethnic chauvinism of the pan-Slavists.

Many of Eurasianism's original advocates, having reconciled themselves to the new regime and returned, perished at its hands in the 1930s. Thereafter the flame was kept alive as the preoccupation of a dissident fringe. Its leading proponent was the ethno-historian Lev Gumilev, son of the poets Nikolai Gumilev and Anna Akhmatova.[4] His extensive writings gave Eurasianism a new, biological twist: Eurasia was not so much a spatial as an ethno-racial entity, in which several distinct *ethnoi* lived harmoniously under the rule of a Russian *superethnos*. The latter was fated to clash, however, with the cosmopolitan universalism of the West. Gumilev's ideas gave a pseudo-scientific veneer to a Soviet countercultural version of race-thinking, repackaging crude prejudices as high-minded doctrine by wrapping them in nebulous terminology of his own devising. Many were drawn to his work because it seemed to square the circle of national and ethnic questions in the USSR: there were supposedly enduring, essential differences between the peoples of the former Russian empire, and yet there was a paradoxical unity in their separateness – and that unity was apparently the benign side effect of Russian dominance. The USSR was simply the latest form taken by a biologically determined destiny.

Amid the disorientations of *perestroika* and especially during the 1990s, Gumilev's ideas gained a huge audience. They seemed to offer a non-Communist justification for Russia's continued sway over its periphery, implicitly allowing readers to see the loss of empire as a temporary bump on a path foreordained as much by genetics as by geopolitics. Long after Gumilev's death in 1992, his books continued to be issued in enormous print-runs. By some measures, he could be classed as the most influential intellectual of the post-Soviet era, implanting in several million readers a set of deterministic, essentialist ideas about ethnicity and history.

Yet the version of Eurasianism that has come increasingly to the fore in the twenty-first century is a slightly different complex of ideas. Often dubbed 'neo-Eurasianism', it shares some features with its predecessors: like the original Eurasianists, its adherents focus on Eurasia as a unit, seeing it as fundamentally opposed to the West along a number of axes; they also share Gumilev's belief in the distinctive, essentialized characteristics of ethno-national groups. But unlike its precursors, neo-Eurasianism is concerned above all with the contemporary struggle against Western-led globalization, which is imposing a homogenizing liberal cosmopolitanism on the world. Indeed, in terms of its real intellectual lineage this new strand of thinking ironically owes less to Russians than it does to Western reactionary thinkers of the twentieth century: interwar theorists of geopolitics such as Carl Schmitt, figures from the French New Right such as Alain de Benoist, and pundits like Samuel Huntington, with his idea that the new century would be shaped by a 'clash of civilizations'.

Neo-Eurasianism's most energetic promoter has been Aleksandr Dugin, who became perhaps the emblematic Russian public intellectual of the 2010s: part media-friendly expert on geopolitics, part bearded Dostoevskian mystagogue.[5] His career is in its own way a chronicle of Russian nationalism's development. The son of a military intelligence officer, Dugin was closely involved in the birth of the Russian far right in the 1980s and early 1990s, including the anti-Semitic organization 'Pamyat' (Memory) and the National Bolshevik Party. At the same time, he produced assorted ramblings on esoteric philosophy, in which he paid tribute to the Nazis' obsession with the occult. Up to the mid-1990s, few besides cranks were interested in these ideas. But the deep unpopularity of Yeltsin's liberal reforms, and the continuing humiliation of Russia's loss of status on the world stage, opened a way into the mainstream for nationalist themes. Dugin, too, worked his way into the corridors of power, becoming adviser to Duma speaker Gennady Seleznev and writing a primer on the *Foundations of Geopolitics* (1997) that was well received by the Russian military.

In the new century, Dugin expanded his reach and readership, producing several documentaries and publishing dozens of books with sonorous titles such as *The Fourth Political Theory* (2009) and *In Search of the Dark Logos* (2013). He became an increasingly frequent presence on Russia's TV screens, wheeled out to comment on the deeper reasons for the incompatibility between Russia and the West. With the Ukraine crisis, Dugin shot to international prominence, identified by many Western analysts as the geopolitical brains behind the annexation of Crimea and the most influential voice urging Putin to go still further. In July 2014 he called on the president to step up Russian intervention in eastern Ukraine – Dugin made a point of calling it 'Novorossiia' – in order to 'save Russia's moral authority'.[6] This merging of geopolitical designs with quasi-religious language was typical. Fittingly, in 2015, Dugin became chief editor of 'Tsargrad', a TV station funded by the Orthodox Christian oligarch Konstantin Malofeev and set up to wage an Orthodox information jihad against Western liberalism.

Dugin's thinking has all along been an eclectic, thoroughly postmodern mix, but the core of it is geopolitical, deploying various warmed-over concepts to explain Russia's inevitable confrontation with the West. From British geographer Halford Mackinder he picked up the idea of Eurasia as a 'world-island', a zone with Russia at its heart that served as 'the geographical pivot of history'. From Carl Schmitt he adopted a binary opposition between land powers and sea powers ('tellurocracies' and 'thalassocracies'), which would always ultimately set Russia against the West. These constructs not only offered an alternative to the Westernizing stance of the Yeltsin and early Putin governments, they also made Russia's continued dominance of the countries surrounding it a matter of geographical and historical necessity. What might have been mere imperial nostalgia was reformatted as deep strategic thinking. Moreover, Dugin seemed to provide an explanation for the frustrations and ultimate failure of the Westernizing policy, and a higher purpose for the independent course Russia would now have to plot. Freed of the delusion that it might join the liberal West, the country could now pursue its Eurasian destiny.

In the 2010s, Dugin's thinking and that of the Putin government have seemed increasingly aligned – leading some Western pundits to dub Dugin the Kremlin's *éminence grise*, or even 'Putin's Rasputin'. But how much credence should we give to this? It's true that Duginite terminology has crept into public discourse and official media. To a large extent, though, this has been part of a wider turn to the right under Putin, who over time has come to see himself as a defender of conservative values. (Not coincidentally, the thinkers and historical figures most commonly cited by the Kremlin in the 2010s have included the White émigré philosopher Ivan Il'in and the hard-line tsarist prime minister Pyotr Stolypin.) The Kremlin's domestic policies have certainly been informed by a desire to defend Orthodox 'civilization', whether through laws against 'gay propaganda' or through persecution of non-Orthodox religious minorities; but again, such virulent prejudices are part of the standard repertoire of the right, in Russia as elsewhere.

Even in the realm of geopolitics, where one would expect to see Dugin's stamp most clearly, the real significance and reach of the Eurasianist idea is far from obvious. During the 1990s and 2000s, Russian foreign policy documents made repeated references to 'Eurasia', but in the early 2010s the emphasis on 'Eurasian integration processes' became much stronger, thanks to the formation of the Eurasian Customs Union in 2010 and the Eurasian Economic Space in 2012. Two years later, these were combined into the Eurasian Economic Union, a single market and customs union comprising Russia, Kazakhstan, Belarus, Armenia and Kyrgyzstan.* Yet there is no necessary relationship between these state-level trade pacts and the 'civilizational' murmurings of Dugin and his ilk. Even though Russia is by far the largest state in the Eurasian Union, the Union itself is nonetheless a deal made by sovereign governments, rather than an imperial *Anschluss* in the name of Russian ethno-national chauvinism. More to the point, regional trade pacts of this kind have become the global norm, from the EU's single market to NAFTA, from Mercosur to the Trans-Pacific Partnership. The Eurasian Union is in that sense very much a late-comer, and remains distinctly underdeveloped relative to its peers.

There are, moreover, many different routes by which any kind of Russian government – liberal or conservative, far right-influenced or social-democratic – might have arrived at the same idea, none of which would have to involve a deeper commitment to neo-Eurasianist thinking. Indeed, the notion that the former USSR should constitute a privileged sphere of influence for Russia

---

* Ukraine had been invited to join, but it quickly became clear that the EU Association Agreement and the Russian-dominated 'Eurasian' project were mutually exclusive; this put the Ukrainian government in a quandary, setting the stage for Yanukovych's U-turn and the Maidan protests in 2013.

has been a constant in the country's foreign policy since 1991, and a desire for a kind of post-Soviet Monroe Doctrine to be applied to Eurasia has been shared across the political spectrum. In 2003, for example, Anatoly Chubais – architect of the free-market reforms of the 1990s – called for Russia to establish a 'liberal empire' over the former USSR: he argued that the country 'can and must do all it can to grow, strengthen and consolidate its leading positions in that part of the planet over the next 50 years'.[7]

The escalating confrontation with the West may have struck some in Russia as proof of Dugin's 'civilizational' diagnoses – the Ukraine crisis and its aftermath finally confirming Russia's definitive exclusion from, and opposition to, the Western liberal order. But neo-Eurasianist ideas had no role in producing the confrontation itself. As we have seen, from the start of the post-Soviet era there were fundamental mismatches in power and strategic interests between Russia and the West. These generated tensions that steadily rose over time, and notably burst into the open in Ukraine in 2003–04, Georgia in 2008 and Ukraine again in 2013–14, among other places.

Ultimately, the recent prominence of Dugin and neo-Eurasianism should be understood as an attempt to fill the ideological void left by the pro-Western idea, as Russia's relations with the West have deteriorated, and to give a larger meaning to the country's geostrategic position and physical location. In that sense, neo-Eurasianism is less a cause of the Kremlin's policy shifts than a symptom of Russia's continuing dilemmas, less a coherent ideology than a mindset that seeks to make virtues out of the country's uncomfortable situation. Its rise has certainly given oxygen to some ugly ideas, and these have made a difference to the tone of Russian policy as well as the rationales offered for it. But neo-Eurasianist fantasies cannot in themselves transform the conditions in which that policy is made.

———

Russia's geopolitical options will, for a considerable time to come, be shaped by a series of constraints. Several of these arise from dynamics internal to Russia, but the most important ones emerge at the global level. The most decisive feature of Russia's present-day role in the world, which flows into every calculation it makes, is its intermediate status. Too big to be digested by regional blocs such as the EU, too independent of the US to admit into NATO, Russia is nonetheless no longer powerful enough to form a significant geopolitical or economic pole on its own. It occupies a difficult mid-category between the hegemonic US and a rising China on the one hand, and on the other a handful of large states, chiefly Brazil and India, that are rapidly leaving behind their status as 'developing countries'. It remains the world's largest country, with a still numerous and well-educated population, not to mention a nuclear arsenal and significant natural resources. But at the same time its economic weight is dwindling: in 2015, its GDP per capita was around a sixth that of the US, a fifth that of Germany and a quarter of the OECD average; it was roughly level with Brazil's and Turkey's, and only fractionally higher than China's.

The tremendous disparity in power and resources between Russia and the West translates directly into their uneven military capacities. Russia is currently the world's second-largest exporter of weapons, and still has one of the largest armies in the world in terms of personnel, though many of the troops are teenage conscripts. Yet in 2015, for example, Russia devoted about a tenth as much money to its armed forces in absolute terms as the US did, and only slightly more than the UK; in per capita terms, it spent somewhat less than Germany or Greece. All told, its 2015 military budget came to around 8 per cent of the total for NATO as a whole, almost 70 per cent of which was spent by the US alone.[8] What enables Moscow to pose a military threat to its neighbours at present is not so much the scale or strength of its armies as its readiness to use force quickly and decisively. But this is more a trap than an advantage, a short-term tactical manoeuvre that has significant strategic downsides in the long term. The possibility that Moscow will use force against them has already driven Russia's neighbours further into NATO's embrace, and propelled a new round of the arms race for which Russia is still more poorly equipped than in Soviet times.*

Russia's intermediate status is to some extent a residue of the USSR's role as the core of what used to be called the Second World, and of Moscow's decades-long effort to construct a systemic alternative to the capitalist West. The possibility of Russia leading such a challenge today seems remote: it lacks both the will and the means to reconstitute anything like the USSR, and has little desire to impose its ideology, its political system or its economic model on states further afield. For all the concern about the tentacular spread of Putin's influence, its actual capacity to shape political outcomes has proved negligible to non-existent – the 2016 US elections very much included. The Kremlin does indeed seek to convert whatever leverage it possesses into concrete advantages, and this can involve all kinds of tactics, from discreet negotiations to loud threats to covert meddling. But the resources at Russia's disposal are fewer than in 1917 or 1945, and the forces likely to oppose it are far stronger.

But what does Russia want? The question of what kind of power it will be in future – whether it wants to reconstitute the USSR in new 'Eurasian' packaging or not, whether it sees itself as funda-mentally opposed to the West or merely distinct from it – cannot be separated from the environment in which it will have to operate. At present, the interstate order is dominated by a single power, the US, which retains a massive military advantage over all other powers; despite the phenomenal rise of China, the US also remains the nerve centre of the global economy, its currency and government bonds the world's default repositories of value.

---

* Part of the reason for this is phenomenal corruption in military procurement, which makes Russian weapons systems among the most expensive on the planet.

Over the past decade, however, the idea of a coming 'multi-polar' or 'polycentric' international order has become widespread among many international-relations theorists, as they try to discern what kind of world might emerge after the 'unipolar' moment of US dominance has passed.[9] The idea has long been popular in Moscow, and over time has been built into the thinking of Kremlin strategists. First mooted under Primakov in the mid-1990s, it remained a wishful fiction for the rest of that decade. But Washington's expanding aggressions after 9/11 were read as early signs of trouble for the single superpower. The deepening disaster of Western interventions in the Middle East since then, and Russia's apparent ability to alter the course of the conflict in Syria in 2015–16, were similarly seen in Moscow as further portents of US decline.

It does seem reasonable to assume that US hegemony will eventually come to an end, just as the Pax Britannica did before it, and it makes sense to debate what kind of world order will follow. Will China slide smoothly into the role of next global hegemon? Are we headed for an anarchic system in which no single power takes the place of the US? Or will the world to come do away with the dominance of states altogether, replacing that pattern with a world-market society?[10]

These alternative scenarios would have very different consequences, for Russia as for everyone else. From Moscow's perspective, a Chinese-dominated world would be unlike the US-dominated order in one especially crucial respect: Russia would now share an extensive land border with the single superpower. If the PRC became the US of the twenty-first century, would Russia become its Mexico – economically integrated with and strategically subordinated to the giant next door? The world-market scenario poses a different kind of threat: a dilution or even dissolution of state sovereignty that might produce all kinds of socio-economic or even territorial fragmentation, turning existing nation-states into little more than cartographic fictions.

In an anarchic world system, meanwhile, the dilemmas presented by China's gravitational pull would also apply, but Russia's strategic options would be more varied – as would the dangers it would potentially confront. In theory, it could act as a kind of 'swing power', aligning with Washington, Beijing or another state to tilt the scales against any given opponent. By forming such alliances, it could carry out its own version of nineteenth-century great-power balancing. Or might it function as a kind of global buffer zone between China and the West, its strategic weight deriving from abstention from the great-power conflicts ahead? Either way, this would turn inside out Mackinder's 1904 description of 'Euro-Asia' as the 'geographical pivot of history': there, Russia was pivotal by virtue of being the 'heartland' of decisive historical events – the zone whose fate, from the Mongols to the Romanovs, determined the fortunes of the landmasses around it.[11] Here, Russia would be pivotal precisely by standing outside the main centres of global power and wealth.

For now, however, any post-American world seems a long way off. What happens in this long interregnum depends to a large extent on what the West does, since the basic power imbalance between it and Russia still governs strategic calculations on both sides. This leaves Russia hovering in a kind of geopolitical and historical limbo while the world is reconfigured around it. Yet during this interval Russia itself will not be standing still: several different far-reaching transformations will remake it from within.

It is the year 2028, and Russia is ruled by a neo-feudal, Orthodox monarch who has built a vast stone wall around the country, 'to cut us off from stench and unbelievers', broken only by the pipelines taking oil to Russia's clients abroad. Meanwhile an elite state security force terrorizes the population, driving around Moscow's ten-lane expressways in red 'Mercedovs' and checking the rouble's exchange rate against the yuan on the screens of their 'news bubbles'. This is the 'New Russia' of Vladimir Sorokin's *Day of the Oprichnik*, which combines futurological fantasy with grim reminders of the past. Published in 2006, the book was strikingly prescient in foreseeing the increasingly patriotic direction in which the Putin system was tending, and in imagining a re-run of earlier confrontations with the West. It was also revealing in its geopolitical assumptions and projections: 'New Russia' had become little more than a space of transit – a country traversed by, if not reduced to, pipelines and roads ferrying raw materials and goods between China and the West, peripheral to and dependent on both.

One of the things that made Sorokin's dark satire compelling was that it extrapolated recognizable features of the present – including Russia's already excessive reliance on natural resources, which today account for three-quarters of the country's exports.[12] This structural feature of the Russian economy has been long in the making, and seems destined to linger, imposing powerful limits on the country's ability to choose its own path in future.

The prolonged economic disaster of the 1990s and then the recovery in the 2000s somewhat obscured the relentless progress of a shift that had been under way since at least the 1960s. Soviet industrial growth, after achieving impressive results at tremendous human cost in the 1930s and 1940s, began to slow in the postwar period, the pace dropping even as equipment began to age. A rash of oil discoveries in Western Siberia allowed the Brezhnev regime and its successors to paper over the problems caused by this slow-down; instead of a deeper recession, the USSR experienced a long period of stagnation. But the relief afforded by energy exports also brought a growing dependency on them: they went from 16 per cent of total exports in 1970 to 47 per cent in 1987.[13] In the mid-1980s, a drop in oil prices starved the USSR of funds just as Gorbachev was implementing his economic reforms, and the low continued for much of the 1990s, making the post-Soviet slump longer and deeper than it might otherwise have been. Prices only really recovered at the end of the century, in time for Putin to benefit from them. Since then, Russia has become ever more dependent on energy exports: they accounted for half of total exports in 2000, and that share rose steadily each year until Western sanctions began to bite in 2015.[14] Gas, too, has become an important export product, as have precious metals and ores, with which Russia is also abundantly endowed.

The disproportionate size of the primary-resource sector spells trouble for the rest of the economy, as the experience of many other countries has shown, from the 'Dutch Disease' of the 1960s to the impact of oil on Nigeria and Venezuela. The over-whelming weight of lucrative export commodities causes currency appreciation that leaves other industries uncompetitive; this makes it all the more difficult to pursue alternative strategies for growth, deepening the 'resource trap'. The Russian government has repeatedly affirmed the need to diversify the economy – perhaps the peak expression of this being Medvedev's 2009 pseudo-manifesto 'Forward, Russia!', which bemoaned the country's 'primitive resource economy, chronic corruption, our outmoded habit of relying on the government, on foreigners or on some "almighty teachings" to solve our problems – on anything except ourselves'.[15]

Yet for all that, the 'modernization' Medvedev promised never materialized, and Russia's dependence on natural resources if anything increased, especially under the impact of the 2008 economic crisis and the post-Ukraine sanctions. After tumbling for several years, oil prices stabilized in 2016 and then crept up again, and in the meantime the economy had staged a modest recovery, allowing the Kremlin to balance its budgets once more. But growth estimates for the next few years are sluggish at best – in late 2017, the OECD projected Russian GDP growth of under 2 per cent for 2018–19[16] – and certainly insufficient to fund a wholesale overhaul of the economy. Based on current trends, it's hard to imagine Russia's resource dependency being reduced by much before the 2028 of Sorokin's fantasy.

What this means in turn is that Russia will struggle to regain its Soviet-era niche as an industrial power. The transition to capitalism brought an accelerated deindustrialization, increasing Russia's reliance on energy exports without producing any compensating gains in employment. After all, one of the features of what is known as the 'fuel-energy complex' is that it requires considerably less labour than manufacturing. Russia's already diminished industrial sector has thus far been unable to attract the levels of investment, domestic or foreign, that would be required for a new burst of growth, making a Chinese- or East Asian-style 'miracle' hard to imagine, even if those earlier successes hadn't already raised the levels of global competition still higher.* Unable to compete with China and the Asian Tigers on wages, Russia similarly lags behind its wealthier Western peers in terms of high-value goods – another instance of the country's difficult middle position. Having moved up the economic hierarchy over the course of the twentieth century, Russia is likely to find itself stuck several rungs lower down in the twenty-first.

A further constraint on Russia's ability to manoeuvre – and one that is equally symbolic of its global downsizing – is its dwindling population. It is still the ninth most populous country in the world, with 143 million inhabitants at the time of the last census, in 2010. But that number is set to contract inexorably in the coming years: the UN Population Division envisages a drop to 133 million by 2050, and to 126 million by 2050; by the start of the next century it could be as low as 124 million. This will push Russia down the global demographic hierarchy: the fourth most populous state in the world in 1950, by 2050 it will have

---

* The fact that so many of Russia's wealthy park their money overseas rather than investing it in Russia itself not only fuels tremendous domestic inequalities, but also puts the country at a strategic disadvantage internationally.

fallen to fifteenth place, overtaken by Pakistan, Ethiopia and Egypt, among others.[17]

This decline represents the continuation of a demographic crisis that first became visible in 1992, when deaths exceeded births in Russia for the first time since the Second World War. Between the collapse of the USSR and the last census, in fact, Russia's population decreased by an estimated 5.4 million, an annual average drop of 284,000. The traumas of transition played a role in this shrinkage, the post-Soviet years bringing a spike in mortality and a collapse of the public health infrastructure. But its roots are broader and deeper, going back to longer-term processes of demographic change over the course of the twentieth century – declining birth rates linked to urbanization and rising female literacy – as well as the catastrophic losses inflicted by war and Stalinist terror.[18] Though the Kremlin has enacted some pro-natalist policies, offering monetary incentives for women to have more children, these efforts will not be enough to offset the decline, much less reverse it.

The shrinking of the population is taking place at the same time as a marked 'greying' of Russian society: an increase in the proportion of middle-aged and elderly citizens. In 2010, 18 per cent of the total population was over sixty – the same proportion as in the US, and considerably less than in Germany or Japan. The UNPD's projections show the percentage rising over the coming decades, to 29 per cent by 2050, levelling off thereafter until 2100 – an estimated 36 million people. This would again be a share similar to the US's, but less than Germany's or Japan's.

In Russia as elsewhere, such trends imply a formidable rise in the 'dependency ratio', requiring more and more of the resources generated by a shrinking workforce to be deployed in caring for pensioners. In much of the developed world, these looming pension obligations – the term 'overhang' is frequently used – have been used to justify increases in the retirement age. But in Russia there are powerful moral arguments against such moves:

shorter life expectancy and higher mortality rates than in the West or Japan, say, mean that the Russian pension system is already heavily subsidized by men and women who do not survive to retirement age. Shifting back the date at which they can claim their pensions would compound the injustice of working lives already too harsh to last as long as they should. While Russian demographic trends in many ways echo those of the industrialized world, then, there are differences that seem likely to make the politics of the ageing society particularly sharp-edged there – perhaps demanding an even more thorough rethinking of the country's economic model.

The only thing that can mitigate the effects of a contracting and ageing population is a substantial inflow of migrants. According to a 2006 study led by Anatoly Vishnevsky, Russia's leading demographer, in order simply to maintain Russia's population at its present level, an annual net migration of around 900,000 people would be required until 2024, rising to an average of more than 1.2 million migrants a year until 2050. Accurate figures are hard to come by, but at present migrants in Russia probably number around 12 million, something like 8 or 9 per cent of the total population. Given Russia's low birth rates, if the population does stay steady, an increasing proportion of it will be recent immigrants: according to Vishnevsky's team, as much as 15 per cent by 2025, and 35 per cent by 2050.[19]

At present, most migrants to Russia come from former Soviet republics – the lion's share from Tajikistan, Uzbekistan and Kyrgyzstan. If anything like the influx required to offset natural population decline materializes, it will rapidly alter Russia's demographic make-up. Migrant workers have already been subjected to chauvinist harassment and violence, and one could be forgiven for fearing there is worse to come, given the tide of empowerment and impunity the far-right has been riding in recent years. It is likely, too, that what is already an ethnically segmented workforce will settle into a more permanent ethnicized social hierarchy, like those of other post-imperial societies such as France or Britain. But at the same time, the very processes and experiences of migration might just propel a rethinking – however halting or partial – of the idea of Russianness itself, giving a stronger emphasis to civic components over ethnic ones, and allowing that idea to inhabit a wider range of forms and meanings.

Of course, Russia's ethnic composition is already hugely varied: the country is home to more than 150 different officially recognized groups, from the 5 million-strong Tatars, descendants of the Mongol armies, to the Nganasans of the Arctic, who number barely 900, and from the myriad mountain peoples of the North Caucasus, predominantly Muslims, to the shamanic Udege of the Amur River basin, among scores of others. But taken together, these groups comprise only a small part of the total: Russians have always been the dominant group within their multi-ethnic empire, and today account for 80 per cent of the population. Even with substantial immigration, it will be some time before ethnic Russians lose their overall majority status. But since fertility rates among non-ethnic Russians are at present higher than among ethnic Russians, the demographic preponderance of ethnic Russians will visibly be eroded soon enough, regardless of migratory flows. The social consequences of this demographic tilt are hard to predict. Politically, its effects bleed into those of another critical matter that will confront Russia in the years to come: the 'national question', which beset the USSR in its final days, and which reared its head once more during the Ukraine crisis.

Nominally, Russia today is a federation, comprising eighty-three territorial 'subjects' – plus two more since 2014, with the Republic of Crimea and the city of Sevastopol – each of which possesses its own constitution, government, parliament and flag. On paper, these entities have many of the attributes of statehood, and only delegate certain powers to the federal centre in Moscow. But the reality is very different: in practice, Russia is a highly centralized polity, and the country's supposedly federal subunits are little more than administrative divisions within a clear hierarchy – what Putin himself famously called a 'vertical of power'.

This gap between federal form and centralizing substance was present during the Soviet period: the USSR was constitutionally a federation of equally sovereign components, but in reality all major decisions and even many minor ones were made in Moscow. In the early 1990s, however, many of Russia's own subunits gained effective sovereignty, having been encouraged by Yeltsin to 'take as much as they could swallow'. This led to prolonged tussles between the federal centre and regional elites. By 1994, Yeltsin managed to claw back the advantages Moscow had yielded (with the single exception of Chechnya, which refused to sign a new Federal Treaty, having already declared full independence).

Putin carried on and completed the centralization Yeltsin had begun, imposing his 'vertical of power' through administrative reorganization – adding a layer of federal plenipotentiaries and eliminating elections for regional governors – and by tightening the purse strings: in 2001, tax revenues were split roughly fifty-fifty between Moscow and the regional governments, but by 2008 the federal government's share had risen to 70 per cent. The effect of this was to reinforce and widen the gap between federal form and content. In the words of political scientist Brian Taylor, Putin 'saved Russian federalism by killing it'.[20]

Chechnya's bid for independence marked a critical turning point in this process: the war Yeltsin unleashed in that republic in 1994–96 was supposed to 'restore constitutional order' by bombing the Chechens back into line. The deaths of tens of thousands of Chechnya's civilians and the flattening of its cities were intended as an example, showing the rest of Russia's federal subunits what would happen to those who made further breakaway attempts. Here again Putin completed Yeltsin's work, bringing Chechnya back into the federal fold by imposing on its beaten population a dictatorship loyal to the Kremlin, and in particular to Putin personally.

Yet the force of the example was undermined only a few years later, when after the 2008 war with Georgia, Russia recognized the independence of South Ossetia and Abkhazia. Whatever was left of Russia's commitment to the idea of territorial integrity vanished completely during the Ukraine crisis, when it first annexed Crimea after a hasty referendum supervised by 20,000 Russian troops, and then backed secessionist rebels in the Donbass, while making intermittent noises about absorbing eastern Ukraine's Russian-speaking territories. It seems unlikely that this second annexation was ever seriously considered: the Kremlin was instead floating the idea of reconstituting 'Novorossiia' in order to push the West to back down. The attempt clearly failed; but at the same time, it opened up once more the Pandora's box of separatisms Russia had apparently fought so hard to keep shut since the early 1990s.

Could Russia itself go the way of the USSR? The Soviet Union had separated into fifteen pieces that were already distinct, like the drifting apart of shards from an ice sheet that was already cracked. By a historical irony, the hollow constitutional structures of the USSR came to be filled with national content that helped pull the Union apart. But the equivalent scenario for Russia would mean a much more dramatic reconfiguration of the map: several of the country's non-Russian components – the likeliest candidates for secession – are not located at its edges, but embedded within a huge landmass with a predominantly Russian population. Another wave of secessions would mean balkanization on a continental scale, turning much of Eurasia into a territorial jigsaw. This, of course, was the nightmare that had haunted Russia in the early 1990s, only to melt away in the wreckage of Grozny. Among many Russians and Westerners alike, the conventional assumption is that this devastation was the price of maintaining the country's territorial integrity. The same reasoning has been used to legiti-mate the strangulation of federalism ever since: any power Moscow surrenders to the regions, the argument goes, will ultimately encourage them to peel away entirely.

Yet this logic rests on false premises. The first is that Chechnya's example would have been emulated by other regions. Though there were certainly nationalist currents among a number of Russia's ethnic minorities, the struggles between Moscow and the regions mostly revolved around the distribution of resources; only in Chechnya did a serious and sustained push for sovereignty develop.[21] The second false premise is that since ethno-nationalism killed the USSR, any further manifestations of it would spell the same outcome for Russia. Again, nationalism framed in ethnic terms certainly did play a role in the unravelling of the Soviet system, but to attribute an entire, epoch-making set of events to this single cause makes little sense. Moreover, it neglects the critical contribution of Soviet elites, who deserted the system in droves, helping themselves to pieces of the planned economy on the way, and thus accelerated its disintegration. The important point here is that the existence of the USSR's formally sovereign republics provided those elites with plenty of other states to desert to. From this self-interested point of view, the subunits of Russia itself – especially the landlocked ones, far removed from borders with other countries and hence from alternatives to alliance with or dependency on Moscow – are nowhere near as attractive a proposition.

But more telling still is the assumption of a necessary connection between federalism and ethno-national separatism. More than a quarter of Russia's subunits are 'republics' or 'autonomous regions' named after ethno-linguistic groups indigenous to them. Russian nationalists see the very existence of these federal forms as a threat – Dugin, for example, has proposed their elimination.[22] Yet in many of these 'ethnic' republics, the majority of the population are ethnic Russians. In these cases, 'national' names and symbols are a historical residue of conquest and assimilation, rather than a draft project for independence. Elsewhere, to be sure, the titular nationalities are numerically dominant: in the Sakha Republic in the Far East, in Tatarstan, in much of the North Caucasus. But as a whole, the non-Russian peripheries are far outweighed by the country's enormous ethnic Russian core: 60 per cent of the territory, containing 80 per cent of the population. This raises an important, largely unspoken question: if the reason for killing federalism is to suppress ethno-national separatism, why does this in practice overwhelmingly apply to territories that are inhabited by ethnic Russians?

One answer is that the actual purpose of Russia's anti-federal federalism is to maintain centralized political control over a vast territory, while shielding that power from democratic scrutiny at all levels. It is telling, from this point of view, that Putin's response to the Beslan atrocity of 2004, when Chechen Islamist militants seized a school and took hundreds of children hostage – only for the vast majority of those present to be killed when Russian security services stormed the building – was to do away with elections for regional governments nationwide. If there were any connection between state security and degrees of local democracy, Putin should have done the opposite. In 2014, though Moscow furnished the rebellion in the Donbass with arms and troops, and to begin with noisily promoted the rebels in official media, its enthusiasm had limits: besides being pro-Russian, the Donbass militias were strongly anti-oligarchic, a stance that might potentially have popular appeal well beyond eastern Ukraine. When it came to it, the Kremlin knew which side of the barricades it would rather be on.

These reflexive moves to defend the system of 'imitation democracy' demonstrated that the real threat posed by federalism was not ethnic rebellions but political ones. Annexing the Donbass would have set an especially dangerous precedent, and not only in terms of international law: it would also have shown Russia's own majority Russian-speaking regions that rebellion paid off, and that they could seize control of their own destinies through acts of political will. This was a potential chain reaction the Kremlin had to avoid setting off at all costs. The underlying risk here was not territorial fragmentation, but democratization.

At bottom, the main points of contention in Russia's federal system derive not so much from dynamics of ethnic difference as from disagreements over the distribution of power and resources, and over the forms and character of government itself. The federal structure provides an arena in which those questions can be raised and contested, which is why the Kremlin must keep it under tight control. But as long as the federal forms exist, the possibility of such an opening remains. Political scientist Andrei Zakharov has called Russian federalism a 'dormant institution'.[23] What would happen if it were someday to awaken?

The guiding assumption of Kremlin policy for the past three decades has been that real federalism leads to national disintegration. But this purposely ignores the potentially democratizing aspect of federalism: its capacity to make government reflect and cater to the specificities of each territory, and to bring power closer to its popular sources. In other words, though it is often seen as a challenge to the existence of Russia itself, federalism could be the site of a struggle between different kinds of Russia. It may be that the possibilities for a more democratic polity there will demand a revival and deepening of federalism, rather than its continued sedation. This might not redraw the map of Russia, as is commonly feared, but instead open up new roads for the country to travel.

The place where all of the forces and factors laid out here converge – where geopolitical pressures meet demographic trends, where economic constraints collide with questions of federal form – is in the political system. What kind of country Russia will be depends partly on who rules it, and for whose benefit. Although its options are limited in various ways, much nonetheless hangs on how the current system of government in Russia, whether under Putin or his eventual successors, responds to changing circumstances. The spike in tensions with the West has for the moment given the Putin-led system a certain amount of leeway, since it can ascribe many of the problems the country experiences to foreign enemies. It helps that this is not, factually speaking, incorrect: the sanctions regime imposed in 2014 prolonged Russia's economic difficulties, and in the wake of Crimea and especially the 2016 US elections, Western media, pundits and politicians eagerly fanned a hostility to Russia that mirrored the hysteria of Russia's own pro-Kremlin outlets.

But how long can this state of affairs continue? In the immediate future we are unlikely to see a dramatic improvement in relations between Russia and the West. Again, some kind of rapprochement is certainly possible. But beneath the mutual suspicions of the present, and beyond any potential pragmatism in future, the interests of the two parties remain fundamentally incompatible, and the West has no reason to alter its course. Ironically, its very hostility to Russia, and to Putin in particular, is the best insurance policy for the 'imitation democratic' regime. For now, the entwinement of the Kremlin's domestic fortunes with its foreign policy choices is a bonus for the system rather than a liability. But although the Kremlin's appeals to patriotism have enjoyed a certain success among the Russian public, they have also been largely defensive in nature, producing reflex responses rather than generating positive attachments or ideals. For the Putin-led system, nationalism is a default ideology, a means of legitimizing the continuation of its power, rather than an active political project. This is what has made its propaganda ultimately so hollow: the frenzied imaginings of state media are a sign of the weakness of their grip on the popular imagination, rather than its strength.

Yet the very character of the system – a predatory, authoritarian elite presiding over a vastly unequal society – will inevitably generate further social tensions, sparking recurrent crises which cannot all be resolved by patriotic mobilizations or military adventures abroad. 'Imitation democracy', and the post-Soviet capitalism it was built to defend, will no doubt be able to survive many upheavals. But it seems unwise to bet on its indefinite continuation, given the speed with which the USSR unravelled over the course of 1991, and the Romanov empire before it a century ago. These twin spectres of disintegration have haunted the imagination of Russia's rulers since the fall of Communism, and they stalk the corridors of the Kremlin still, waiting for another of those rare, history-shattering moments when they can take on solid form.

Epilogue

To say the Russian presidential election of 18 March 2018 was not a contest would be a gross understatement. Everything unfolded according to the Kremlin's script. Not only was Putin re-elected by a crushing majority – he won 77 per cent of the vote, compared with a mere 12 per cent for his nearest rival, the Communist Party's Pavel Grudinin – there was also a satisfactory 68 per cent turnout, dispelling Russian officialdom's fears that voter apathy would undermine the legitimacy of the poll. Independent observers reported hundreds of instances of ballot-stuffing and other irregularities, but these were breezily dismissed by the Central Election Commission.[1] To no one's surprise, Putin effortlessly secured another six-year term, extending his hold on power to 2024.

This was a textbook demonstration of the 'imitation-democratic' system in action: all the appearances of electoral democracy with none of the uncertainty. But while the vote posed no problems for the regime internally, it took place at a moment of dramatically heightened external tensions. Two weeks beforehand, on 4 March, the attempted murder of former Russian spy Sergei Skripal and his daughter in the quiet English town of Salisbury had immediately been blamed on his former paymasters in the Kremlin. The weapon apparently used, a nerve agent based on the Novichok series developed in the USSR in the 1970s and '80s, made Russian involvement somewhere along the line – whether by the state or by non-state actors – seem likely. Amid the uproar and conspiracy-mongering the incident unleashed, no convincing explanations were advanced as to why the Russian state would make an already bad situation so much worse for itself. But the mysterious facts of the case were soon enough overshadowed by its consequences: sanctions, tit-for-tat expulsions of diplomats, closures of consulates. The incident drove already dismal relations between Russia and the West to new lows, making it even harder to imagine a normalization in the near future.

This combination of domestic stability and turmoil on the international front set the parameters for the immediate future of Russia's imitation-democratic system. But behind the events of early 2018 lay a larger question concerning the system's long-term prospects. It had been prompted, ironically, by the very ease and inevitability of Putin's victory. Since it had long been obvious what the outcome of the 2018 elections would be, in the run-up to the vote many minds in Russia turned to the end of Putin's forthcoming term, when he would be constitutionally ineligible to run again. Who or what would succeed him in 2024? An eerie temporal displacement seemed to have taken place, in which confirmation of Putin's domestic political dominance was shadowed by thoughts of its eventual end, his success in the present trailed by his future departure from the scene.

What had appeared on the horizon – still distant for now, but visible – would be the end of an era. By early 2018 Putin had effectively outdone Brezhnev's eighteen years as Soviet leader. Assuming he makes it through to the end of his new mandate, Putin will have ruled his country for a quarter of a century. Perhaps a fifth of the Russian population has never known any other leader. In that sense, the very length of Putin's hold on power has amplified the problem of succession common to many political systems – how to manage the transition from one leader to the next without massive instability or infighting? Putin's age and apparent good health seemed to add another layer to the problem: what is a figure who has held such power supposed to do in his retirement? Will Putin be content to retreat gracefully to the wings, leaving the stage clear for a new imitation-democratic figurehead? And – very much related – will his successor be able to shield him from prosecution as Putin himself protected Yeltsin?

But while the urge to speculate about Putin's personal fate is understandable, it is ultimately misguided. It prolongs the tendency to focus excessively on this single individual in order to understand Russia. The imitation-democratic system has indeed functioned much to the satisfaction of Russia's elite with Putin in charge. But it is fundamentally a *system* – that is, a set of power structures and political practices that has enabled Russia's particular, post-Soviet form of capitalism to thrive. That system can certainly continue with another person at its summit – perhaps less smoothly, or perhaps better. The question we should really be asking, in fact, is not whether the system can function without Putin, but how long it can keep functioning in the same way, regardless of who is in charge.

On the one hand, the outlook for the regime is not especially positive. In addition to a tense international climate and unfavourable economic winds, it must struggle against its own internal exhaustion. The centralizing, neoliberal energies of Putin's first presidential term have been left behind, and while the patriotic turn after 2012 and the confrontation with the West have certainly helped firm up the regime's domestic support, they can't fully compensate for a lack of other motivating ideas or projects. On 1 March 2018 Putin made a speech laying out his governing agenda for the next six years. The part that drew the most attention in the West, inevitably, was his announcement – complete with video animations – of shiny new hypersonic missiles that could get around Western defence systems. The speech also promised increased spending on infrastructure, health care and education, as developmental priorities for the coming decade. But promises of this kind have been made before and proven hollow. The 2018–2020 budget, approved in December 2017, certainly envisaged no significant alterations to the system's current priorities. If anything, the new government will most likely simply continue the budgetary austerity and 'optimization' measures of the past few years, which have brought school and hospital closures even as wages and pensions lag well behind inflation.[2] In mid-June 2018, just as the country was distracted by the start of the World Cup, the government announced a plan to increase the retirement age, by five years for men and eight for women – highly regressive moves which the Kremlin may yet have cause to revisit.

Overall, the Putin government's aim seems to be an inertial scenario. It has entered what political scientist Yekaterina Schulmann has called 'calorie-conservation mode'.[3] There is an obvious danger here, of aimless drift or complacent decline. Systems that lose their sense of purpose can rapidly end up losing their grip on power, too, overtaken by emergencies they lacked the imagination or energy to foresee. One possible scenario, indeed, is that the imitation-democratic system will gradually run out of steam, so hollowed out from the inside that it eventually crumbles at the slightest popular pressure.

Yet even once toppled, such regimes have often returned in near-equivalent forms, like strange political revenants. In Georgia, for example, Mikheil Saakashvili's administration eventually replicated many of the authoritarian behaviours of the Shevardnadze government it displaced; further afield, in Egypt, after the hopeful upheavals of Tahrir Square Sisi took up many of the despotic habits of Mubarak. These repetitions were what Dmitri Furman had in mind when he gave his book on imitation democracies the title *Spiral Motion* – identifying the tendency, across the post-Soviet space and far beyond, for countries governed by such regimes to find themselves circling through variations on the same governmental theme.[4] Furman's compelling metaphor describes a default scenario – and implies that something substantive has to change for a country to break out of the spiral and forge a new trajectory.

Russia's imitation democracy is capable of reproducing itself whether Putin is in charge or not. If it is to be replaced by something substantively different, an alternative to the system as a whole will have to coalesce – not just an anti-Putin who can take the current president's place. This is no small task, and it would have to be the work of a large-scale movement rather than an elite plot or a few scattered individuals. Yet it's possible that Putin's fourth term might provide an opportunity for such a project to begin to take shape. A period of stasis for the ruling system could also be a valuable interval for those ranged against it, allowing Russians to think about what kind of country might await them beyond imitation democracy, and to imagine what a future without Putin would look like.

– June 2018

Acknowledgements

THE SEEDS OF THIS BOOK were sown by many years of discussions with colleagues and comrades at *New Left Review*. Thank you to the editor, Susan Watkins, for her consistent engagement with and support for the project, and for allowing me time off from my editorial duties there to explore the ideas that have gone into it. Thank you also to Kheya Bag, Rob Lucas, Johanna Zhang and Daniel Finn, and to Dylan Riley for his incisive comments on the *NLR* article that eventually became Chapter 3 of this book. I'm also tremendously grateful to Perry Anderson for his close critical reading of the final manuscript, and for suggestions which improved it significantly.

A preliminary version of Chapter 3 was presented at the Centre for Baltic and East European Studies at Södertörn University in October 2011, and I thank the participants in the seminar for their comments, in particular Zhanna Kravchenko for her thoughtful response; thanks also to Irina Sandomirskaia for offering encouragement, and to Sven Hort for making my stay at CBEES possible. Others of the book's arguments were first sketched out in essays for the *London Review of Books*, and I'm grateful to Mary-Kay Wilmers for the chance to write regularly on

Russian themes there, and to Daniel Soar and the rest of the editorial staff. Likewise to Keith Gessen and *n+1*, for organizing a symposium on Ukraine in the autumn of 2015 which helped focus my thinking on the Maidan and its aftermath.

Thanks must also go to Sean Guillory and Kyle Shybunko for their perceptive and helpful comments on the final manuscript; to Ilya Budraitskis, Aleksei Penzin and Maria Chekhonadskikh for many insights and conversations about contemporary Russia; to Leo Hollis, my editor at Verso, and to Jacob Stevens, Mark Martin, Anne Rumberger and everyone else at Verso for helping this book into the world. The list of family, friends and colleagues who have at various times been subjected to my ramblings on Russia is lengthy, and I apologize in advance for leaving anyone out – but for now, thank you to my parents, Michael Wood and Elena Uribe; to Gaby Wood, Ava Turner and Beatrice Turner; to Patrick Wood and Holly Chatham; to Richard Reeve, Surmaya Talyarkhan, Andrew Greenall, James Tindal, Susan Jones, Rob Leech, James Leech, Michael Frantzis, David Klassen, Chase Madar, Rachel Nolan, Brian Kuan Wood and Alexander Zevin.

Finally, but most importantly, thank you to Lidija Haas. With incredible patience, intelligence and editorial skill, she helped me rethink this book several times over, and offered unflagging encouragement throughout. Much more than making this book possible, she makes my life immeasurably better.

Notes

Introduction

1 ' "No Putin, No Russia," Says Kremlin Deputy Chief of Staff ', *Moscow Times*, 23 October 2014.

Chapter 1: The Man and the System

1 The most comprehensive accounts of Putin's background and career are Steven Lee Myers, *The New Tsar: The Rise and Reign of Vladimir Putin*, New York 2015, and Fiona Hill and Clifford Gaddy, *Mr Putin: Operative in the Kremlin* [revised and expanded edition], Washington, DC 2015. Other works I have drawn on here include Masha Gessen, *The Man without a Face: The Unlikely Rise of Vladimir Putin*, London 2012; Anna Arutunyan, *The Putin Mystique*, London 2014; Angus Roxburgh, *The Strongman: Vladimir Putin and the Struggle for Russia*, London 2011; Allen Lynch, *Vladimir Putin and Russian Statecraft*, Washington, DC 2011; and Richard Sakwa, *Putin: Russia's Choice* [second edition], London 2008.

2 Vladimir Putin et al., *First Person: An Astonishingly Frank Self-Portrait by Russia's President*, London 2000.

3 Putin et al., *First Person*, pp. 69–70, 79.

4 Gleb Pavlovsky, 'Putin's World Outlook: Interview by Tom Parfitt', *New Left Review*, 88, July–August 2014, p. 56.

5 Quoted in Hill and Gaddy, *Mr Putin*, p. 149.

6 Gessen, *Man without a Face*, p. 120; Myers, *New Tsar*, pp. 78–79.

7 The fullest account is in Gessen, *Man without a Face*, ch. 5.

8 Hill and Gaddy, *Mr Putin*, p. 159; Myers, *New Tsar*, pp. 80–81. It seems plausible that Warnig and Putin met in Dresden in the 1980s – as Myers points out, there are group photographs from the time in which they both appear – but the two men deny it.

9 The Russian sociologist Alena Ledeneva has written the indispensable books on this theme: *Russia's Economy of Favours*, Cambridge 1998; *How Russia Really Works*, Ithaca, NY 2006; and *Can Russia Modernise?*, Cambridge 2013.

10 Myers, *New Tsar*, p. 126.

11 Historical prices from the US Department of Energy's Energy Information Administration.

12 Figures from Rosstat, World Bank and Vladimir Popov, 'Russia Redux?', *New Left Review* 44, March–April 2007.

13 Gryzlov's aphorism has become proverbial in a slightly different form – 'Parliament is no place for discussions.' For his original wording, see 'Boris Gryzlov izbran spikerom Gosdumy chetvertogo sozyva', *Leningradskaia pravda*, 29 December 2003.

14 Daniel Mitchell, 'Russia's Flat Tax Miracle', Heritage Foundation website, 24 March 2003; Thomas Friedman, 'Russia's Last Line', *New York Times*, 23 December 2001.

15 The best picture of the post-Soviet oil industry is Thane Gustafson, *Wheel of Fortune: The Battle for Oil and Power in Russia*, Cambridge, MA 2012.

16 Myers, *New Tsar*, pp. 114–15. The thesis and the 1999 article are lucidly analysed by Harley Balzer in 'The Putin Thesis and

Russian Energy Policy', *Post-Soviet Affairs*, vol. 21, no. 3, 2005, pp. 210–25.

17 See Andrew Barnes, *Owning Russia: The Struggle over Factories, Farms, and Power*, Ithaca, NY 2006, p. 218.

18 Gerald Easter, 'Revenue Imperatives: State over Market in Post-Communist Russia', in Neil Robinson, ed., *The Political Economy of Russia*, Lanham, MD 2012, p. 62.

19 Steven Levitsky and Lucan Way, 'The Rise of Competitive Authoritarianism', *Journal of Democracy*, vol. 13, no. 2, 2002; Andrew Wilson, *Virtual Politics* New Haven 2005; Olga Kryshtanovskaia and Stephen White, 'Putin's Militocracy', *Post-Soviet Affairs*, vol. 19, no. 4, 2003.

20 Luke Harding, *Mafia State*, London 2011; Karen Dawisha, *Putin's Kleptocracy*, New York 2014.

21 An English-language condensation of Furman's arguments can be found in 'Imitation Democracies', *New Left Review* 54, November–December 2008, pp. 28–47. Furman was Russia's leading comparative scholar on post-Soviet politics; for a comprehensive account of his life and work, see Perry Anderson, 'One Exceptional Figure Stood Out', and 'Imitation Democracy', *London Review of Books*, 30 July 2015 and 27 August 2015.

22 David Hoffman, *The Oligarchs: Wealth and Power in the New Russia*, New York 2011 [revised and updated edition], p. 358.

Chapter 2: Faces of Power

1 The full US list is accessible at www.treasury.gov; The EU list is at www.consilium.europa.eu, the UK's at hmt-sanctions. s3.amazonaws.com, with Russians listed under 'Ukraine (Sovereignty)'. On Gunvor, see 'Secretive Russian Gunvor becomes number 3 oil trader', Reuters, 31 October 2007; and on the Rotenbergs and Sochi, see 'Putin Friend Bags at Least 21 Russian Olympic Contracts', Bloomberg, 27 March 2013.

2   For a rather excitable version of this argument, see Dawisha, *Putin's Kleptocracy*.

3   'KGB Inc', *Economist*, 20 January 2005; Nick Paton Walsh, 'Meet the chief exec of Kremlin Inc', *Guardian*, 5 July 2005; Peter Finn, 'Kremlin Inc. Widening Control Over Industry', *Washington Post*, 19 November 2006; Michael Specter, 'Kremlin, Inc.', *New Yorker*, 29 January 2007; Catherine Belton and Neil Buckley, 'Steeled to succeed – Ivanov sets out his tough vision for Russia's future', *Financial Times*, 19 April 2007.

4   Anders Åslund, 'Russia's New Oligarchy', *Washington Post*, 12 December 2007.

5   'The rise of state capitalism', *Economist*, 21 January 2012; 'Putin stands by state capitalism', *Financial Times*, 30 January 2012; Vladimir Gelman, 'Russia's crony capitalism: the swing of the pendulum', *openDemocracy*, 14 November 2011; Anders Åslund, 'Russia's Neo-Feudal Capitalism', *Project Syndicate*, 27 April 2017.

6   Olga Kryshtanovskaia, *Anatomiia Rossiiskoi elity*, Moscow 2004, p. 302; Hoffman, *The Oligarchs*, p. 113.

7   Figures from Barnes, *Owning Russia*, p. 56, Table 3.1.

8   Clear accounts of this process are offered by Kryshtanovskaia, *Anatomiia Rossiiskoi elity*, pp. 307–18, and Steven Solnick, *Stealing the State: Control and Collapse in Soviet Institutions*, Cambridge, MA 1998, ch. 7.

9   Quoted in Hoffman, *The Oligarchs*, pp. 185, 192–93, 203.

10 A lucid account of the privatization process is in Barnes, *Owning Russia*, ch. 4.

11 Barnes, *Owning Russia*, pp. 75–76, Tables 4.1 and 4.2.

12 Barnes, *Owning Russia*, p. 77.

13 Figures from Hoffman, *The Oligarchs*, p. 205.

14 For a detailed account of the struggles for ownership and control in the oil industry, see Gustafson's *Wheel of Fortune*.

15 Aven quoted in Peter Reddaway and Dmitri Glinski, *The Tragedy of Russia's Reforms: Market Bolshevism against Democracy*,

Washington, DC 2001, p. 603; Khodorkovsky in Hoffman, *The Oligarchs*, p. 232.

16 Thomas Remington, *The Politics of Inequality in Russia*, Cambridge 2011, p. 107.

17 Serguey Braguinsky, 'Postcommunist Oligarchs in Russia: Quantitative Analysis', *Journal of Law and Economics*, vol. 52, May 2009, pp. 307–349. I thank the author for his generosity in sharing the data on which he based his analysis; the political conclusions I draw from it are entirely my own.

18 Gustafson, *Wheel of Fortune*, p. 294.

19 See Gustafson, *Wheel of Fortune*, p. 136 and Hoffman, *The Oligarchs*, p. 398.

20 Hoffman, *The Oligarchs*, pp. 315, 318, 319–20; Barnes, *Owning Russia*, pp. 112–13.

21 Quoted in Reddaway and Glinski, *Tragedy of Russia's Reforms*, p. 494.

22 Kryshtanovskaia, 'Finansovaia oligarkhiia v Rossii', *Izvestiia*, 10 January 1996.

23 Hoffman, *The Oligarchs*, p. 360.

24 David Woodruff, 'The Expansion of State Ownership in Russia: Cause for Concern?', *Development and Transition*, July 2007; Neil Buckley and Arkady Ostrovsky, 'Back in Business – How Putin's Allies Are Turning Russia into a Corporate State', *Financial Times*, 19 June 2006.

25 Alena Ledeneva, *Can Russia Modernise?*, p. 69.

26 Reddaway and Glinski, *Tragedy of Russia's Reforms*, p. 599.

27 Barnes, *Owning Russia*, p. 170.

28 William Tompson, 'Putin and the "Oligarchs": A Two-Sided Commitment Problem', in Alex Pravda, ed., *Leading Russia: Putin in Perspective*, Oxford 2005, p. 190.

29 Gustafson's *Wheel of Fortune*, ch. 7, offers one of the most judicious accounts of the Yukos affair.

30 Woodruff, 'Expansion of State Ownership in Russia'.

31 Tompson, 'Putin and the "Oligarchs"', p. 190.

32   See for instance 'The Making of a Neo-KGB State', *Economist*, 25 August 2007, and Lilia Shevtsova, 'The Next Russian Revolution', *Current History*, October 2012; both cited in David Rivera and Sharon Werning Rivera, 'Is Russia a Militocracy?', *Post-Soviet Affairs*, vol. 30, no. 1, 2014, p. 28.

33   Olga Kryshtanovskaya and Stephen White, 'Putin's Militocracy', *Post-Soviet Affairs*, vol. 19, no. 4, 2003, p. 293, Table 1; Kryshtanovskaya and White, 'The Sovietisation of Russian Politics', *Post-Soviet Affairs*, vol. 25, no. 4, 2009, p. 295, Table 2.

34   Andrei Soldatov and Irina Borogan, *The New Nobility: The Restoration of Russia's Security State and the Enduring Legacy of the KGB*, New York 2011; Vladimir Sorokin, *Day of the Oprichnik* [2006], New York 2010.

35   Viktor Pelevin, *The Sacred Book of the Werewolf* [2004], London 2008, pp. 218–20.

36   These objections are laid out meticulously by Rivera and Rivera, 'Is Russia a Militocracy?', to which I am indebted.

37   Olga Kryshtanovskaya and Stephen White, 'The Rise of the Russian Business Elite', *Communist and Post-Communist Studies*, 38 (2005), pp. 302–303.

38   Barnes, *Owning Russia*, pp. 177–78 and Kryshtanovskaia, *Anatomiia rossiiskoi elity*, pp. 356–57.

39   Kryshtanovskaya and White, 'Rise of the Russian Business Elite', p. 305.

40   Kryshtanovskaya and White, 'Rise of the Russian Business Elite', pp. 300–301.

41   Viktor Cherkesov, 'Nel'zia dopustit', chtoby voiny prevratilis' v torgovtsev', *Kommersant*, 9 October 2007; on the 'Tri Kita' case, see Ledeneva, *Can Russia Modernise?*, pp. 182–188.

42   Ledeneva, *Can Russia Modernise?*, pp. 99–100.

43   Thanks to Sean Guillory for this point.

44   Ledeneva provides a helpful glossary in *Can Russia Modernise?*, pp. 273–80.

45   'Rodnia vo vlasti', *Kommersant-Vlast'*, 24 September 2007; 'Kak

ustroilis' deti chinovnikov, i chto v etom nepravil'nogo', *Meduza*, 30 May 2017.

46 Levada Tsentr, 'Institutsional'naia korruptsiia i lichnyi opyt', 28 March 2017.

47 Dmitri Trenin, *Getting Russia Right*, Washington, DC 2007, p. 10.

48 Shaun Walker, 'Russian cellist says funds revealed in Panama Papers came from donations', *Guardian*, 10 April 2016.

Chapter 3: Red Bequests

1 'The long life of *Homo sovieticus*', *Economist*, 10 December 2011; Svetlana Alexievich, 'Nobel Lecture: On the Battle Lost', 7 December 2015.

2 Masha Gessen, *The Future Is History: How Totalitarianism Reclaimed Russia*, New York 2017.

3 Leon Trotsky, *The Revolution Betrayed* [1937], trans. Max Eastman, New York 2004, pp. 180–81.

4 Figures in this paragraph from Basile Kerblay, *Modern Soviet Society*, London 1977, p. 127; and Constance Sorrentino, 'International comparisons of labor force participation, 1960–81', *Monthly Labor Review*, February 1983, p. 25, Table 1.

5 Donald Filtzer, *Soviet Workers and De-Stalinization*, Cambridge 1992, pp. 201–2.

6 T. H. Rigby, *Communist Party Membership in the USSR, 1917–1967*, Princeton 1968, p. 53.

7 Figures from David Lane, *The End of Social Inequality?*, London 1982, p. 117.

8 The lower figure is taken from Kryshtanovskaia, *Anatomiia rossiiskoi elity*, p. 17; the higher is from Mikhail Voslensky's *Nomenklatura: Anatomy of the Soviet Ruling Class*, London 1984, p. 95.

9 See Filip Novokmet, Thomas Piketty and Gabriel Zucman, 'From Soviets to Oligarchs: Inequality and Property in Russia,

1905–2016', *NBER Working Paper* 23712, August 2017, p. 69, Figure 10c.

10 Bertram Silverman and Murray Yanowitch, *New Rich, New Poor, New Russia: Winners and Losers on the Russian Road to Capitalism*, Armonk, NY 1997, p. 46.

11 World Bank, 'Russia: Targeting and the Longer-Term Poor', May 1999, Volume I, p. 6, Table I; Reddaway and Glinski, *Tragedy of Russia's Reforms*, p. 302.

12 Leonid Gordon and Eduard Klopov, *Poteri i obreteniia v Rossii v 90-kh. Tom 2: Meniaiushchaiasia zhizn' v meniaiushcheisia strane: zaniatost', zarabotki, potreblenie*, Moscow 2001, pp. 360–61, Table 16.5.

13 Figure quoted in Serguei Oushakine, *The Patriotism of Despair*, Ithaca, NY 2009, p. 8.

14 Figures from Linda Cook, *Postcommunist Welfare States: Reform Politics in Russia and Eastern Europe*, Ithaca, NY 2007, pp. 65, 82, 190, 79.

15 World Bank, 'Russia: Targeting and the Longer-Term Poor', May 1999, Volume II: Annexes, pp. 15–17.

16 For a perceptive survey of these questions, see Jane Zavisca, *Housing the New Russia*, Ithaca, NY 2012.

17 Barnes, *Owning Russia*, pp. 87–104; see also Grigory Ioffe, Tatyana Nefedova and Ilya Zaslavsky, *The End of Peasantry? The Disintegration of Rural Russia*, Pittsburgh 2006, pp. 107–29.

18 Ovsei Shkaratan, 'Sotsial'noe rassloenie v sovremennoi Rossii: drama raskolotogo obshchestva', *Mir Rossii*, no. 1, 2004, pp. 43–44, tables 5 and 7, gives a figure of 3 to 4 per cent for entrepreneurs, traders and private farmers, but half of these did not own a firm, so the number of owner-businessmen is much smaller.

19 For a compelling ethnographic sketch of post-Soviet traders, see Caroline Humphrey, *The Unmaking of Soviet Life*, Ithaca, NY 2002, pp. 85–90.

20 A memorable sociological description of this milieu can be found in Vadim Volkov, *Violent Entrepreneurs*, Ithaca, NY 2002; see

also Mark Galeotti's definitive history *The Vory: Russia's Super Mafia*, New Haven 2018.

21 Svetlana Stephenson, *Crossing the Line*: *Vagrancy, Homelessness and Social Displacement in Russia*, Aldershot 2006, p. 114.

22 Humphrey, *The Unmaking of Soviet Life*, pp. xvii–xviii.

23 Peter Nolan, *China's Rise, Russia's Fall: Politics, Economics and Planning in the Transition from Stalinism*, Houndmills 1995, p. 124, Table 5.2.

24 Figures cited in Cook, *Postcommunist Welfare States*, p. 64, Table 2.2.

25 Figures from World Bank Open Data website.

26 Karine Clément, *Les ouvriers russes dans la tourmente du marché*, Paris 2000, p. 111.

27 Shkaratan, 'Sotsial'noe rassloenie v sovremennoi Rossii', p. 43.

28 For a valuable account of this phase, see Sue Bridger, Rebecca Kay and Kathryn Pinnick, *No More Heroines? Russian Women and the Market*, London and New York 1996, ch. 1.

29 Tatiana Zaslavskaia, survey of May–November 1993, cited in Silverman and Yanowitch, *New Rich, New Poor, New Russia*, p. 54.

30 Quoted in Bridger, Kay and Pinnick, *No More Heroines?*, p. 51.

31 Andrew Stickley, Olga Kislitsyna et al, 'Attitudes Toward Intimate Partner Violence Against Women in Moscow, Russia', *Journal of Family Violence*, vol. 23, 2008, pp. 447–56; see also Lynne Attwood, ' "She was asking for it": rape and domestic violence against women', in Mary Buckley, ed., *Post-Soviet Women: from the Baltic to Central Asia*, Cambridge 1997, pp. 99–118.

32 Shkaratan, 'Sotsial'noe rassloenie v sovremennoi Rossii', p. 31.

33 Lev Gudkov and Boris Dubin, 'Bez napriazheniia' (1993), in *Intelligentsiia: Zametki o literaturno-politicheskikh illiuziiakh* [1995], 2nd ed., St Petersburg 2009, pp. 152–53.

34 Thanks to Irina Sandomirskaia for alerting me to this document.

35 Andrei Sinyavsky, *The Russian Intelligentsia*, New York 1997, p. 22.

36 Sinyavsky, *Russian Intelligentsia*, pp. 12–13.

37 Viktor Erofeev, 'Zhivoe srednevekov'e', *Obshchaia gazeta*, 14–20 January 1999; my attention was drawn to this text by Clément, *Les ouvriers russes dans la tourmente du marché*, p. 212.

38 Gudkov and Dubin, 'Ideologiia besstrukturnosti' (1994), in *Intelligentsiia*, p. 279.

39 Mikhail Ryklin, 'Medium i avtor: O tekstakh Vladimira Sorokina', afterword to Vladimir Sorokin, *Sobranie sochinenii v dvukh tomakh*, vol. 2, Moscow 1998, p. 744.

40 Figures from Stephen Crowley, 'Labour Quiescence in Post-Communist Russia', National Council for Eurasian and East European Research paper, October 2000, p. 3.

41 On this history, see Sarah Ashwin, 'Russian Trade Unions: Stuck in Soviet-Style Subordination?', in Craig Phelan, ed., *Trade Union Revitalisation: Trends and Prospects in 34 Countries*, Oxford 2007, pp. 319–32; and Paul Kubicek, *Organized Labor in Postcommunist States*, Pittsburgh 2004, ch. 5.

42 Novokmet, Piketty and Zucman, 'From Soviets to Oligarchs', p. 59, Figure 7d.

43 Income figures from Rosstat database.

44 Author's calculations based on Rosstat data.

45 Author's calculations based on 2005 Rosstat data.

46 Tullio Buccellato and Tomasz Mickiewicz, 'Oil and Gas: A Blessing for the Few: Hydrocarbons and Inequality within Regions in Russia', *Europe-Asia Studies*, vol. 61, no. 3, 2009, pp. 385–407.

47 Grigory Ioffe and Zhanna Zayonchkovskaya, 'Immigration to Russia: Inevitability and Prospective Inflows', *Eurasian Geography and Economics*, vol. 51, no. 1, 2010, p. 108.

48 For poll data on attitudes to migrants in Moscow during the 2000s, see Tatiana Yudina, 'Labour Migration into Russia: the Response of State and Society', *Current Sociology*, vol. 53, no. 4, 2005.

49 Figures from Gustafson, *Wheel of Fortune*, p. 391 citing Rosstat data.

50 'Issledovanie RBK: skol'ko v Rossii chinovnikov i mnogo li oni zarabatyvaiut', *RBK*, 15 October 2014.

51 Valeria Korchagina, 'Intelligentsia Shifts to Support Putin', *Moscow Times*, 30 November 1999.

52 Kirill Medvedev, *It's No Good: Poems, Essays, Actions*, trans. Keith Gessen et al, New York 2012, p. 115.

53 Medvedev, *It's No Good*, p. 132.

54 For a systematic account of the Putin government's gradual extension of control over the media, see Masha Lipman's chapter 'The Media and Political Developments', in Stephen Wegren, ed., *Return to Putin's Russia: Past Imperfect, Future Uncertain*, Lanham, MD 2013.

55 Nelli Romanovich, 'Dikhotomiia otnosheniia intelligentsiia k vlasti', *Sotsiologicheskie issledovaniia*, 1, 2009, p. 70.

56 'Burgeoning bourgeoisie', *Economist* Special Report, 14 February 2009, p. 4.

57 Gryzlov, Surkov and Putin all quoted in Thomas Remington's excellent article, 'The Russian Middle Class as Policy Objective', *Post-Soviet Affairs*, vol. 27, no. 2, 2011, pp. 109, 105.

58 Tatiana Maleva, 'Sotsialnaia politika i sotsialnye straty v sovremennoi Rossii', in *Kuda prishla Rossiia?*, Moscow 2003, pp. 102–13; further studies by Natalia Tikhonova, Olesia Yudina and Liudmila Khakhulina cited in Remington, 'Russian Middle Class', pp. 98–99.

59 Cited in Remington, 'Russian Middle Class', p. 98.

60 Evgeniia Pishchikova, *Piatietazhnaia Rossiia*, Moscow 2009, p. 164.

61 Natalia Tikhonova, 'Maloobespechennost' v sovremennoy Rossii', *Sotsiologicheskie issledovaniia*, No. 1, 2010, p. 10.

62 Nemtsov quoted in Reddaway and Glinski, *The Tragedy of Russia's Reforms*, p. 632; Camdessus in Paul Kubicek, *Organized Labor in Postcommunist States*, Pittsburgh 2004, p. 226, n. 115.

Chapter 4: An Opposition Divided

1   Cliff Kupchan, 'Putin's New Constraints', *New York Times*, 13 March 2012; see also 'The reawakening of Russian politics', *Financial Times*, 4 March 2012; Luke Harding, 'Putin has six more years to draw level with Brezhnev', *Guardian*, 4 March 2012.

2   Gideon Rachman, 'The ice is cracking under Putin', *Financial Times*, 6 February 2012; 'The beginning of the end of Putin', *Economist*, 3 March 2012.

3   'The shock of the old', *Economist*, 20 January 2005.

4   On these movements, see Karine Clément et al, *Ot obyvatelei k aktivistam: Zarozhdaiushchiesia sotsial'nye dvizheniia v sovremennoi Rossii*, Moscow 2010, pp. 150–83.

5   Simon Pirani, *Change in Putin's Russia: Power, Money and People*, London 2010, p. 164. Other details on the emergence of the new labour movement are drawn from Clément et al, *Ot obyvatelei k aktivistam*, pp. 228–94.

6   Pirani, *Change in Putin's Russia*, p. 169. Urusov was eventually released in March 2013; on his case, see 'Valentin Urusov: A Worker's Struggle', *Sean's Russia Blog*, 25 January 2013.

7   Figures from Remington, *Politics of Inequality*, pp. 207–8; and the Rosstat website.

8   On Rubtsovsk, see Karine Clément et al, *Gorodskie dvizheniia Rossii v 2009–2012 godakh: na puti k politicheskomu*, Moscow 2013, pp. 278–312. The same book has detailed accounts of mobilizations in Khimki, Kaliningrad and elsewhere, on which I have also drawn in this chapter.

9   Ben Judah, *Fragile Empire: How Russia Fell In and Out of Love with Vladimir Putin*, New Haven 2012, p. 147.

10 Artemy Magun et al, 'The Russian Protest Movement of 2011–2012: A New Middle-Class Populism', *Stasis*, 1, 2014, pp. 160–91.

11 'Opros na prospekte Sakharova 24 dekabria', Levada Centre, 26 December 2011.

12 Masha Gessen, 'It's not just the Russian middle class in revolt – this is a true mass movement', *Guardian*, 3 March 2012.

13 For a moving personal account of the impact of official homophobia, see Masha Gessen, 'As a gay parent I must flee Russia or lose my children', *Guardian*, 11 August 2013.

14 Details on these and other FBK investigations are available in English and Russian on the FBK website, fbk.info.

15 For data and a map of the 12 June protests, see '12 iiunia na ulitsy vyshlo bol'she liudei, chem 26 marta. Karta protestov "Meduzy" i "OVD-Info". Samye polnye dannye', *Meduza.io*, 13 June 2017.

16 Konstantin Voronkov, *Aleksei Navalnyi: Groza zhulikov i vorov*, Moscow 2012, p. 65.

17 Voronkov, *Aleksei Navalnyi*, p. 68.

18 Per Leander and Alexey Sakhnin, 'Russia's Trump', *Jacobin*, 11 July 2017.

19 For versions of this argument, specifically directed against Leander and Sakhnin's article, see Ilya Budraitskis, Ilya Matveev and Sean Guillory, 'Not Just an Artifact', *Jacobin*, 1 August 2017 and Kirill Medvedev and Oleg Zhuravlev, 'The Base and Navalnyi: How Can the Left Work with the Anti-Corruption Movement?', *LeftEast*, 17 August 2017.

20 Partiia Progressa, 'Programma', 8 February 2014; available at partyprogress.org. The party was originally set up by some of Navalnyi's followers in 2012 as People's Alliance, and was renamed in 2014.

21 On the healthcare reform protests, see for example 'Vrachi vzialis'' za lechenie sistemy zdravookhraneniia', *Kommersant*, 2 November 2014. On the *dal'noboishchiki*, see Nikolai Ovchinnikov, 'A voice from Russia's truckers' protest', *openDemocracy*, 9 December 2015, and Ekaterina Fomina, 'We have plenty of reasons to protest apart from Platon', *openDemocracy*, 14 December 2017. On Karelian pensioners, see Anna Yarovaya, 'Extremists by any other name', *openDemocracy*, 31 January 2018.

22 Voronkov, *Aleksei Navalnyi*, pp. 29, 22.

Chapter 5: After the Maidan

1 For a lucid and balanced account, to which the following discussion is indebted, see Andrei Tsygankov, *Russia's Foreign Policy: Change and Continuity in National Identity*, 4th edition, Lanham, MD 2016.

2 Dmitri Trenin, *Post-Imperium: A Eurasian Story*, Washington, DC 2011, p. 75; figures from SIPRI database.

3 Anatol Lieven, *Chechnya: Tombstone of Russian Power*, New Haven and London 1998.

4 Author's calculations from World Bank data (World Development Indicators, retrieved 28 December 2016).

5 On the emergence and rise of the 'New Thinking', see Robert English, *Russia and the Idea of the West: Gorbachev, Intellectuals and the End of the Cold War*, New York 2000.

6 The encounter is described in Dimitri Simes, *After the Collapse: Russia Seeks Its Place as a Great Power*, New York 1999, p. 19.

7 Andrei Kozyrev, 'Russia: A Chance for Survival', *Foreign Affairs*, vol. 71, no. 2, Spring 1992, p. 9.

8 Tsygankov, *Russia's Foreign Policy*, pp. 84, 86, Table 3.6.

9 For a comparison of Russia's economic fortunes with those of other former Soviet states, see Vladimir Popov, 'Russia Redux?', *New Left Review* 44, March–April 2007, especially Figure 2.

10 Dmitri Furman, 'SNG kak posledniaia forma rossiiskoi imperii', in Igor Kliamkin, ed., *Posle imperii*, Moscow 2007.

11 Dmitri Furman was virtually alone in producing systematic comparative studies of all the post-Soviet regimes. Most of these remain unpublished in English, but for an overview see 'Imitation Democracies', *New Left Review* 54, November–December 2008.

12 Tsygankov gives a thorough account of this in *Russia's Foreign Policy*, pp. 97–130.

13 Data from Tsygankov, *Russia's Foreign Policy*, p. 106, Table 4.3 and SIPRI database.

14   For a blow-by-blow description of how the NATO enlargement policy unfolded, see James Goldgeier, *Not Whether But When: The US Decision to Enlarge NATO*, Washington, DC 1999.

15   For a sharp and highly prescient analysis of the implications of NATO enlargement, see Peter Gowan, 'The Enlargement of NATO and the EU', in *The Global Gamble: Washington's Faustian Bid for Global Dominance*, London and New York 1999, pp. 292–320.

16   Address to Johns Hopkins School of Advanced International Studies, 21 September 1993, quoted in Goldgeier, *Not Whether But When*, p. 38.

17   Goldgeier, *Not Whether But When*, pp. 94–5.

18   Goldgeier, *Not Whether But When*, p. 142.

19   Quoted in Goldgeier, *Not Whether But When*, p. 88.

20   Zbigniew Brzezinski, 'Normandy Evasion', *Washington Post*, 3 May 1994.

21   George Kennan, 'A Fateful Error', *New York Times*, 5 February 1997; Thomas Friedman, 'NATO or Tomato?', *New York Times*, 22 January 1997, 'Bye-Bye NATO', *New York Times*, 14 April 1997, 'Foreign Affairs; Now a Word from X', *New York Times*, 2 May 1998.

22   See Svetlana Savranskaya and Tom Blanton, 'NATO Expansion: What Yeltsin Heard', *National Security Archive Briefing Book*, No. 621, 16 March 2018, and the accompanying Document 08, 'Secretary Christopher's meeting with President Yeltsin, 10/22/93, Moscow'.

23   Quoted in Goldgeier, *Not Whether But When*, p. 113.

24   See Sean Guillory, '*Dermokratiya*, USA', *Jacobin*, 13 March 2017.

25   Goldgeier, *Not Whether But When*, p. 112.

26   Strobe Talbott, *The Russia Hand: A Memoir of Presidential Diplomacy*, New York 2002, p. 76. For a fascinating portrait of successive generations of US Russia policy experts, see Keith Gessen, 'The Quiet Americans Behind the US–Russia Imbroglio', *New York Times Magazine*, 8 May 2018.

27 Brzezinski, 'Normandy Evasion'.

28 Peter Conradi, *Who Lost Russia? How the World Entered a New Cold War*, London 2017, p. 123.

29 Conradi, *Who Lost Russia?*, p. 123.

30 Putin et al., *First Person*, p. 169.

31 Vladimir Putin, 'Rossii na rubezhe tysacheletii', *Nezavisimaia gazeta*, 30 December 1999.

32 I have described this in greater detail in *Chechnya: The Case for Independence*, London and New York 2007.

33 Mary Buckley and Rick Fawn, eds, *Global Responses to Terrorism: 9/11, Afghanistan and Beyond*, London and New York 2003, pp. 227–8.

34 'Annual Address to the Federal Assembly of the Russian Federation', 25 April 2005; English translation at en.kremlin.ru.

35 Based on data from the Observatory of Economic Complexity, atlas.media.mit.edu.

36 Tsygankov, *Russia's Foreign Policy*, p. 185.

37 Benjamin Bidder, 'NATO–Russia Relations on the Mend', *Spiegel Online*, 3 November 2010.

38 'NATO chief opposes Russia's security pact proposal', *Reuters*, 17 December 2009; Hillary Clinton, 'Remarks on the Future of European Security', Paris, 29 January 2010.

39 Figures from Trenin, *Post-Imperium*, p. 149.

40 Stefan Lehne, 'Time to Reset the European Neighborhood Policy', *Carnegie Europe*, 4 February 2014.

41 'Joint Declaration of the Prague Eastern Partnership Summit', Prague, 7 May 2009; available at consilium.europa.eu.

42 For a balanced discussion of the stakes around the Association Agreement, see Volodymyr Ishchenko, 'Ukraine's Fractures', *New Left Review* 87, May–June 2014.

43 'Address by the President of the Russian Federation', 18 March 2014; available on Kremlin website.

44 'Kerry condemns Russia's "incredible act of aggression" in Ukraine', Reuters, 2 March 2014.

45 On this history see Galia Golan, *Soviet Policies in the Middle East from World War Two to Gorbachev*, Cambridge 1990, pp. 140–156.

46 Nikolai Kozhanov, *Russia and the Syrian Conflict: Moscow's Domestic, Regional and Strategic Interests*, Berlin 2016, p. 17.

47 Russian Ministry of Economic Development data, cited in Kozhanov, *Russia and the Syrian Conflict*, p. 11, Annex 1.

48 Kozhanov, *Russia and the Syrian Conflict*, p. 2.

49 See for example 'In Syria, militias armed by the Pentagon fight those armed by the CIA', *Los Angeles Times*, 27 March 2016.

50 Maria Zakharova, interview with Ekho Moskvy, 3 November 2015; transcript and audio available at http://echo.msk.ru.

51 'Foreign Minister Sergey Lavrov's interview on the "Sunday evening with Vladimir Solovyev" program on "Russia" TV', Moscow, 10 February 2013; English translation available at www.mid.ru.

52 By far the best analysis of the report and its 'findings' is by Masha Gessen, 'Russia, Trump & Flawed Intelligence', *New York Review Daily*, 9 January 2017.

53 Masha Gessen, 'Russia: The Conspiracy Trap', *New York Review Daily*, 6 March 2017.

Chapter 6: Russia in the World

1 Nikolay Gogol, *Dead Souls*, trans. Robert Maguire, London 2004, p. 283.

2 The Moscow-based SOVA Centre keeps track of such attacks, and issues regular reports on the state of the far right in Russia; see www.sova-center.ru.

3 The literature on Eurasianism is extensive and growing; for an incisive overview, see Marlène Laruelle, *Russian Eurasianism: An Ideology of Empire*, Washington, DC and Baltimore 2008.

4 For a systematic portrait of Gumilev's ideas, and the context in which they developed, see Mark Bassin, *The Gumilev Mystique:*

Biopolitics, Eurasianism, and the Construction of Community in Modern Russia, Ithaca, NY 2016.

5 For portraits of Dugin, see Laruelle, *Russian Eurasianism*, ch. 4; Andreas Umland, 'Aleksandr Dugin's transformation from a lunatic fringe figure into a mainstream political publicist, 1980–1998', *Journal of Eurasian Studies*, vol. 1, no. 2, 2010; on Dugin and Russia's new right more generally, see Charles Clover, *Black Wind, White Snow: The Rise of Russia's New Nationalism*, London 2016.

6 Dina Newman, 'Russian nationalist thinker Dugin sees war with Ukraine', *BBC News*, 10 July 2014.

7 Anatoly Chubais, 'Missiia Rossii v XXI veke', *Nezavisimaia gazeta*, 1 October 2003.

8 Figures from SIPRI database; 2015 is the last year for which full data was available for comparison.

9 See for example Charles Kupchan, *No One's World: The West, the Rising Rest, and the Coming Global Turn*, New York 2012.

10 On the idea of a world-market society, see Giovanni Arrighi, *Adam Smith in Beijing: Lineages of the Twenty-First Century*, London and New York 2007, pp. 7–8.

11 Halford Mackinder, 'The Geographical Pivot of History', *The Geographical Journal*, vol. 23, no. 4, April 1904, pp. 421–44.

12 In 2015, exports of mineral products, metals and precious metals came to $237 billion, out of a total of $317 billon; data from the Observatory of Economic Complexity, atlas.media.mit.edu. The most recent data, from 2016, include a sizeable volume of 'Unspecified' exports, making precise calculations impossible.

13 Boris Kagarlitsky, *Empire of the Periphery: Russia and the World System*, London 2008, p. 292, citing *SSSR v tsifrakh v 1987*.

14 Data on fuel exports from World Bank online database.

15 Dmitri Medvedev, 'Rossiia, vpered!', *Gazeta.ru*, 10 September 2009.

16 *OECD Economic Outlook 2017*, Paris 2017, p. 216.

17 Figures from UN Population Division Database.

18 The most detailed account of this history is Anatoly Vishnevsky et al, *Demograficheskaia modernizatsiia Rossii, 1900–2000*, Moscow 2006.

19 Vishnevsky et al., *Demograficheskaia modernizatsiia Rossii*, pp. 502, Table 22.3, 504 Table 22.5.

20 Brian Taylor, *State Building in Putin's Russia*, Cambridge 2011, p. 113; for figures on tax revenues, see p. 147.

21 I make this argument at greater length in *Chechnya: The Case for Independence*, Ch. 2.

22 Laruelle, *Russian Eurasianism*, p. 118.

23 Andrei Zakharov, *'Spiashchii institut': Federalizm v sovremennoi Rossii i v mire*, Moscow 2012.

Epilogue

1 For a map of violations reported on election day, put together by the independent election monitoring organization 'Golos', see kartanarusheniy.org.

2 See Ilya Budraitskis, 'The Very Best Day', *ArtsEverywhere.ca*, 16 March 2018; and Sergey Zhavoronkov, 'Two Lean Years: Russia's Budget for 2018–20', *Intersection Project*, 6 December 2017.

3 Yekaterina Schulmann, 'How Regime Self-Preservation Could Accidentally Democratize Russia', Carnegie Moscow Center, 14 December 2017.

4 Dmitri Furman, *Dvizhenie po spirali: Politicheskaia sistema Rossii v riadu drugikh politicheskikh sistem*, Moscow 2010.

Index